BUG

"Straight Talk"

By: D. Brown

Printed In the United States of America.

Cover Design by: Angelina Blanks
printdesignsbya@gmail.com

Book Editing & Formatting by: Veronica Lee, Asriel Brown,
& Tonya Brown.

Table Of Contents

Dedications

This book is dedicated to my father, George Brown Jr. my hero.

His hard work along with integrity and his will to love people has motivated me to never give up on life or people!

To my wife Tonya, my angel sent from Heaven to help me, this book is dedicated to your love and to you for making my life so amazing. You are forever the best part of me! I love you.

To BJ, Ebony, Daron and last but not least Asriel, thanks for loving me. Every day I see something to be proud about in you all. You are one of my greatest accomplishments!

And a special thanks to my mother Edwina Greene Abbott for bringing me into this world. Thank you Mama!

Acknowledgements

To Jesus – without your wisdom and revelation none of this would be possible.

*Veronica Lee – Thanks Babygirl for all of your expertise. *Blessed are the pure in heart, for they will see God.* Thanks for putting my heart to paper!

*Angelina Blanks – Thanks for believing in me and for a great book cover.

*Harvest Church Family – Thanks for loving my family so much.

*Dr. Steve Houpe – The wisdom and guidance you have given me has caused true abundance in my life. Thank you Pops!

FOREWORD

I am proud to introduce my Son in the gospel, Darren Brown.

This is an incredible dramatic saga of a person's life that might move you to tears. His early life was filled with extremes; bustling neighborhoods, poverty, hustlers, drug pushers, ladies of the night, and everything else that an underage child shouldn't experience.
As he was forced to progress into an early manhood, he did whatever it took to achieve the so-called American dream of material success. His, is a story of faith and hope. Darren survived despite his desperate circumstances. WOW! The power of prayer and old-fashion acceptance, and the simplicity of love in the gospel. It's clear Darren Brown received more than jailhouse religion. But I do not need to speak for Darren "Bug" Brown—turn the page and let him speak for himself, he's of age.

Dr. Steve Houpe

INTRODUCTION

To the reader, this book is not only about me but you as well. When I began to write this book fear gripped me not wanting to relive the pain that was my life and maybe yours as well, but knowing deep within "Wisdom cries" out as God decrees:

> *For He (God) hath not given me the spirit of fear, but of power, and of love, and of a sound mind.*
> **2 Timothy 1:7. (KJV)**

And soon fear diminished as I quoted this verse, realizing the many obstacles that came up against me gave me the determination and the motivation to continue and finish. The sole purpose of this book as God ordained it is to save a posterity for Him in the Earth and to save lives by a great deliverance! **(Genesis 45:7 KJV)**. Although this book was intended to address men, it is for all mankind. As I look at our communities or cities, and our country, our children are at risk of being extinct before the age of 25; I'm not talking about a third world country, I'm talking about here in the United States. Especially, our young men who are being killed daily at an alarming rate by each other or being incarcerated for decades at a time. We can shift the blame on whomever and whatever we want, but the blame falls directly on us as parents. We can't expect schools, the boy's clubs or any other program or organization to raise our children. And since man has been ordained by God to lead, we have failed miserably, myself included.

As we look around today our inner cities are full of despair, life has no value, murder is as though it were normal in society, and morals have been tossed out the window. No fear of God exists, women and men, young and old give themselves over to sexual lusts and sex with no regard to disease or even death with the outbreak of AIDS in our world. Alcohol and drugs have ravished our inner cities, bringing babies into the world that are unwanted and uncared for not to mention unloved. We have grandmothers in their 30's raising and caring for their daughters and for *their daughter's* daughters as well. If the cycle is not broken we'll see great-grandmothers in their early 50's. As parents, we must take back our children from the influences of the world. We must repent for the lack of responsibility and care that we have shown our seed. The main responsibility falls on man who was called to be the head of the family by God Almighty, who can only produce seed in which the woman carries for up to nine months. So if we're the producer of the seed, it falls on us to take responsibility for training and teaching our seed that they may grow and be fruitful. As I reflect on the pages of this book I'm not discouraged or dismayed because of what I see or hear. I know firsthand the transforming power of Jesus in my own life and my hope and faith causes me to have great expectations for our cities and communities and just as Jesus was…

> *As a root out of dry-ground despised and rejected of men; a man of sorrows and acquainted with grief; and we hid as it were our faces from Him; He was despised, and we esteemed Him not.*
> **Isaiah 53:2a-3 (KJV)**

And as Jesus was, we are today. Facing impossible odds, He survived and triumphed, conceived in scandalous circumstances to an unmarried girl, enduring frequent rejection, beaten and tortured until death, He gave Himself that we may be free in every area of our lives. I believe this great deliverance will start "**NOW**" in the prisons and jails. As roots out of dry ground these men will be soldiers for the Army of God, who won't stop or give in to the world's way of thinking and doing things. God said:

> *Remember ye not the former things neither consider the things of old. Behold I will do a new thing, now it shall spring forth; shall ye not know it, I will even make a way in the wilderness and rivers in the desert. The beast of the field shall honor me, the dragons and the owls; because I give waters in*

the wilderness and rivers in the desert, to give drink to my people, my chosen. This people have I formed myself; they shall show forth my praise.
Isaiah 43:18-21 (KJV)

Why do I think, or should I say know, that this great revival or deliverance will start in prisons? Because God seems to use most powerfully, those who have experienced His greatest love and deliverance. Think about it. Why does there seem to be a systematic plan of genocide for the men of this world, especially our young men? According to the U.S. Bureau of Justice Statistics 2,700,000 adults were incarcerated in U.S. federal and state prisons and county jails at the end of 2011. In addition, there were 90,000 juveniles in detentions in 2011. Furthermore 4,933,667 adults at the year's end were on probation or parole; in total 7,633,667 adults were under correctional supervision (probation, parole, jail or prison). These statistics are unbelievable, but true; more than one in 100 adults in the U.S. are in jail or prison, this is an all-time high that is costing state governments nearly 51 billion dollars a year and the federal five billion more. Out of this total number of prisoners, males make up 92.9% of them. An estimated 200,000 youth are tried, sentenced, or incarcerated as adults every year across the U.S. On any given day 7,500 young people are locked in adult jails and 3,600 in adult prisons! There are 75.2 million young men and women under the age of 18 in this world; we must save our babies! So you see the plan of the powers that be, it's not God's plan—He has called "Man,"—the Almighty God has called us out even with all the negativity concerning our men and our seed in this world. We must recognize the potential that is within our seed and in ourselves.

> ***They are treasures to be redeemed out of darkness:***

> **(Isaiah 45:3)**

God is able to make straight what we have made crooked, I believe in the power of the gospel for it is the *power of God unto salvation to them that believe* **(Romans 1:16a)**. And God will cause a root out of dry ground to grow, just like the mustard seed, by reaching His hand down into the prisons and jails and cause a stirring and an unstoppable army that will do great exploits for God and His Kingdom that will shake and confuse the world.

> ***And they shall reign as kings coming out of prison!***
> **(Ecclesiastes 4:14)**

So come let **Wisdom** cry in your ear! I pray that this book will open up your eyes to the things around you and to the things that are within you. I can only thank God that Jesus died for me. Today I'm living in my best days but it wasn't always this way you see. Because of God's hand I cry out to you. He saved me from myself being incarcerated for 16 years in numerous federal penitentiaries and now I'm free, going on five years. God has been good and as you read this book you will soon see the goodness of God in every situation of my life. As we take this journey some things may be somewhat graphic. This is my life and may God give grace to the hearer that you may see His hand on my life and your life as well. Take special heed to when "**Wisdom Cries**," it will keep you. May God bless the reader and hearer of this book!

Chapter 1
"Bug"

Wisdom Cries:
*"For he said, leave the children alone,
allow the little ones to come to me...*
                    Matthew19:14 (AMP)

Abandonment: *refers to a parent's choice to willfully withhold physical, emotional, and financial support from a minor child. In other words abandonment is when a non-custodial parent fails to fulfill his or her parental responsibilities and chooses not to have contact with the child.*

"Leave the fatherless children, I (God) will preserve them alive."

                    Jeremiah 49:11 (KJV)

Man, "Bubbles" had wet the bed again. That's my sister Stacy. She's sleep. Looking back as I watched the sun rise above my screen torn window trying to keep distance from the wet spot on the bed, my sister and brother lay there sleep. For a moment I begin to think back to when I was four or five. The year was 1969. I used to wear these braces on my legs that went all the way up to my hip and all the way down to my toes. They say my legs were bowlegged real bad. I used to walk on my toes so I wore these braces all the time that kept me from playing with the other kids. I just sat up on the porch. I remember we used to live on 24th and Park where my mother grew up in the house with her brothers and sisters. I'd just sit on the porch all day watching the kids play. My sister was a baby and my brother would run up and down the street along with my cousins. My uncles and aunts sat out on the porch also. Man I used to think, "*I wish I could run like the other kids.*"

My mind bringing me back, I had to wake my brother and sister up—my sister lying in a wet bed. I have to get her up so I can clean her up. I have to find some underwear—they smell like an old basement, but they'll do. I have to wash her up with soap if we have any. The water is cold. I "borrowed" some camphophenic to put on her sores. My momma said its impetigo caused by dirt. In the summer months when the mosquitos were out and biting; she would have to stay in the house but they would still get her. She would scratch and cry. I felt sorry for her so I did what I had to do to take care of her. Let me go walk around the house and see if my mother's here—she's usually not. And sure enough, she wasn't here today either. She's been gone two days now. We finally settled into a house on 51st and Paseo. Moving from house to house, I couldn't understand that, but as a kid what can you say?

My mother, remembering stories about her, my father would tell me all she did was drink Coca-Cola pop and read books. Far cry from that now though. I don't know why she's like that—and why she doesn't care. But I know I have to survive. I have to take care of my brother and my sister.

There's nothing to eat again. I have to run down to Thriftway to "borrow" some more food—or should I say steal. It was one of my routines every two or three days. For some reason, I didn't like stealing but I had to so we could survive. My brother and I went the other day and had to hide our

"...I know I have to survive. I have to take care of my brother and my sister."

sister in the closet. She started to cry but she couldn't run fast enough, so we couldn't take her at the risk of being caught. Somehow every time we went in the store—we were able to get out without getting caught. Well I'll say me because my brother was so scared, he'd stand outside and hold the door when he saw me coming; I'd have lunchmeat and bread, the only thing that I could carry; I was a little buck—but as I look back, I know those people had to have seen me—it was like God had made me invisible to them. Today, if that store were still there, I'd take them the money that I owe them. At that time of my life I really needed that store.

My brother's name is Derrick. We call him D. I'm seven now. My leg braces came off probably when I was about five or six—I can't remember, but it feels good I can run now; man, real fast too. Just thinking about my mom and why she's not here all the time, maybe she's working—**hmmm**, *I don't think so*. We've been hanging around a lot of strange people lately. Every time we go over to somebody's house, its two ladies living together, and one of them is acting like a man. "That's strange." But I'm older now and I understand that it was the spirit of lesbianism. It was introduced to my mother

Chapter 1: BUG

at a young age. She had me when she was 19 and my brother when she was going on 17—he's a year older than me. I'm seven now, he's eight. My sister just turned four. I'm glad we're not moving from house to house around all of those strange women anymore. I didn't like that—and I didn't like my sister around it either.

We're here now, and this house— man, no lights and no gas, but we have candles though. The water is on sometimes but it's not hot. We would sometimes have to wait until it rained just to collect water in pots and pails. We'd hang our clothes outside to be washed or at least rinsed out from the rain. I remember one time being in this house alone with no lights. We played a lot of inventive games—our imaginations ran wild. I often wondered *"where's my daddy at?"* He was here about two weeks ago. He bought us a lot of groceries and asked us where our mother was. We lied to him, because she had been gone for three days. He looked at us kind of strange and said, *"I'll be back."*

Remembering that day when he left, it was late night, about 10 o'clock. Three Caucasian men were knocking at the door.

Peeping out the window not wanting to answer, I was afraid—but not scared. This beating and kicking at the door continued as a man cried, "*I know y'all are in there open up the door—where's my rent money?*" By that time the man had kicked the door in. I'm standing there with my brother and sister behind me with a steak knife in my hand. I probably weighed about 50 pounds at the time. They were three large white men. I was afraid but not scared. "Why did you kick the door down?" I asked. "Where's your mother?" "My mother's not here." I said, as one man walked around the house looking. "I said she's not here! Who's gonna fix the door?" As one of the men laughed, "*she's not here*" came from the other man in the other room. As they walked out the house, my sister cried, my brother cried, and me I'm just mad I couldn't do anything else.

That next week my grandmother came walking up the steps. Lorene McKay—a beautiful woman, older now, had long pretty hair, gray tinted with black, a chiseled face, but pretty. That was Maw-Maw, as I called her. She came up to the door. I couldn't get there fast enough. Opening the door, I was so happy to see her, "Oh Grandma! Maw-Maw!" I said. "Boy, what you doing?" She'd say.

Chapter 1: BUG

Speechless I was just glad she was there. "Where's your mother?" She asked. "She's not here Maw-Maw." She said, "Get some clothes and come on." So we came out with our clothes. As usual they were stinky and dirty and we had holes in our shoes. We hadn't had a pair of shoes for some time now. We couldn't go outside because the kids would make fun of us. So we stayed in the house mostly. When she saw what we were bringing, she said, "Take that stuff back, y'all just come on." She took us as we were.

My grandmother was a stern woman. My mother, I don't think liked her. My brother and sister thought she was really mean; but not me. She was just Maw-Maw. When she took us to her house, I wondered where my father

One of the reasons I believe that I'm alive today is because of (my grandmother) and her prayers. She would always say, "you gone be something boy, you gone be something."

was. I hadn't seen him in a while. But all of a sudden, he just showed up and began living with us at our grandmother's house.

We stayed in a duplex along with my aunt and my cousin. It was seven of us in a 2-bedroom house, but that didn't bother me any, at least now we were safe, clothed and fed. My grandmothers' house was clean. She had her big giant Bible sitting on her dining room table and she would always talk about God. She cussed too though, and drank her Hams beer—but that was Maw-Maw. She taught me everything that my father didn't teach me. She taught me, my brother and sister how to clean, how to cook and how to take care of ourselves. I'm so indebted to her. One of the reasons I believe that I'm alive today is because of her and her prayers. She would always say, "you gone be something boy, you gone be something." Hmm, thanks Grandma.

There was a time in my life when things began to get rough. Growing up I saw my father as a womanizer, a hustler, a gambler and a pimp—in the streets, in the world. He taught me everything that he knew whether good or bad. Then one day he just seemed to disappear again. My grandmother seemed to sugarcoat it a lot. "He'll be back, he'll be home soon." When you're younger you don't understand it. My father was just

Chapter 1: BUG

here and now he's gone. But as I grew older I found out that he had gone to prison.

I noticed that around that time if you lived in the hood, you more than likely knew somebody that was in prison—this somebody just happened to be my father. I remember when we went to visit him, he didn't like that place and he didn't like us coming there either. I told myself that I would have to be self-sufficient. I remember at six years old telling myself that I would never be poor again in my life. Although I had my family I always felt alone. Still wondering why my mother hadn't called. Why after weeks, after months, even years that she hasn't even come by to see how we were doing. My sister cried a lot for her, sometimes my brother did too. Me? I don't know how to feel about that situation. I miss her though. Growing up, I just hoped that my father wouldn't leave like she did.

At 11 years old I started working at an after hour's club called Bulldogs, where they gambled all night, played music and danced. In the streets I had to grow up fast. I saw pimps, whores, or should I say ladies of the evening, hustlers, gamblers,

School and money seemed to compete with one another in my life at this time. murderers and thieves. In this place I saw some things that I shouldn't have seen but that was the only way that I knew how to earn money. I was tired of collecting cans and bottles—it just wasn't enough. I wasn't going to depend on anyone else. My grandmother was there but she was getting older. So I had to look out for myself. In the midst of that, making money, running errands for this club and going to school, it seemed as if everything was working out just right. I had enough money to do the things that I needed and wanted to do. But that life led me to other things. Having my first sexual experience in an afterhours club at 12 years old by a prostitute who performed oral sex on me, my understanding at 12—I'm still trying to grind on girls—it seemed to change my disposition on how I looked at women. Remembering it like it was yesterday, it's strange how some things you can remember 20 or 30 years later. Hmm, a "soul tie" I guess.

School and money seemed to compete with one another in my life at this time. I was getting older and my pops came home, finally out of prison. I had to be in the sixth grade at this time going on 13. I remember my daddy saw me counting a bunch of ones in my room. He just looked and closed the door. A week later, I asked him for $10 for something and he said to me, "When you gone give me my money back?" "What you mean when I'm gone give you the money back?" I replied. "Yea, when you gone give me my money back?" So from then on, everything that I got from my father I literally had to pay back. He bought me my necessities, my school clothes, my shoes, and the things that I needed. Anything extra I bought for myself. He didn't mind me staying out as long as I went to school—he stressed that.

I think about my dad, how I would just look at him and how well he dressed. He was a real clean-cut man. He was always polished, always with class. I miss him now. The wisdom that he's given me has helped me to survive in this world. I thank him for that and I also thank God for my daddy, "George Brown".

As I entered into young adulthood, I met a beautiful young woman in high school who soon turned out to be my wife. When I met her, I told her she would be mine and she laughed at me—guess who got the last laugh? You'll hear about her later. Thinking back, I remember my life really being turned upside down probably about the eighth grade. I came home and my brother and sister were standing in the living room talking. I asked what was wrong and they told me that daddy was crying. They replied that they didn't know why and my grandmother was gone at the time. I went in the room and began to talk to my daddy saying, "daddy what's wrong?" "Oh boy, I just got some things on my mind." At that time I figured he was just concerned about some things that were going on, not understanding that it was a real problem. Not knowing what was going on with my father, I had to go to my grandmother. In talking to her she told me that something had happened to him while he was in prison. I didn't understand it at the moment. What could they have done to him that would cause him to talk to himself and do things that were not normal?

My brother, sister, and I lived with our father's schizophrenia our whole lives.

Chapter 1: BUG

Growing up in that was hard. I grew up fighting a lot because kids made fun of him when he did abnormal things in public. No matter what he was like that was my daddy and I didn't have any problem defending what I loved. Later my daddy sent me to the Golden Gloves. I was a little bitty guy and used to get picked on a lot, used to fight a lot, and used to get beat up a lot. But when I went to the Golden Gloves certain things changed. I got a little older, a little wiser, and a lot tougher. I didn't get picked on anymore. My brother, sister and I lived with our father's schizophrenia (which caused him to worry obsessively) our whole lives. Pops never seemed to get better. There were times when he would go to the hospital. Back then it was a place called Western Missouri. If you went there people would make fun of you saying things like, that's where the crazy people go. So I had to deal with that. That sickness right there was something that I really wanted to understand. It was something that practically killed my father. It's a serious issue.

About 2.4 million Americans or 1.4% of the adult population live with schizophrenia. I don't know if other people can really understand it unless they have experienced living with someone who has it. You have to watch them and take care of them and make sure that they don't hurt themselves. They gave my father pills called "Thorazine." When he took those pills he seemed to calm down. Then a bout would come and he would start to drink heavy; it was one of the telltale signs of him getting worse—he would drink real heavy and I would see my father in a different light. He was a totally different person and I couldn't understand what would cause his mind to become all confused or to imagine that someone was there that wasn't. Now I understand as I've become older that the devil has a lot to do with things of that sort in the spirit realm. That's why I believe that God tells us not to worry about tomorrow. I saw that kill my daddy and I've experienced it in some other areas in my life that we'll get to.

As I embarked upon my senior year, school really wasn't a priority for me. I just went to get by, to make sure I took all the tests and did all the work that I needed to do to pass. I was highly intelligent, that's what my teachers used to tell me. I just believed that I was smart but graduating out of high school and dealing with that life in the world—drugs—which I was introduced to at an early age was causing a lot of problems in my life. I started smoking marijuana in the sixth grade just trying to fit in with the other guys that were popular. One of my best friends at that time introduced me to it. At the time it wasn't nothing, just recreational, didn't really get anything out of it. It just made me hungry and gave me a sense of euphoria. But I saw the effects of it as I went on later in life.

Graduating out of high school I knew I had to do something positive—as I said before I always had to be self-sufficient. I always felt alone for some reason during this time in my life

I always felt alone even though I had family.

even though I had family. Months before my graduation my Maw-Maw's health started to deteriorate. She was a diabetic so I would give her, her insulin, give her a bath, pay all of the bills and do all the things that I needed to do. By then it was just me, Maw-Maw, my brother and my sister. My daddy was there but he wasn't there if you know what I mean. But I knew I had to do something positive in my life. She passed away a couple of months after my graduation. I remember her telling me that she didn't want to die in a hospital. After relaying that message to my father, we brought her home and the next day she passed away. It was 1981. It devastated my family but it also brought us a lot closer together. We ended up moving down into the projects. Chouteau as they call it was a new environment for me. I didn't understand it, but it was home.

I made a decision to go to the Air Force. I told my daddy, "I'm going to try to get stationed close to you so I can always be around you and make sure you're alright." He said, "boy just go on and do you." So I went to the Air Force. A great experience but to be honest it wasn't for me. I didn't like people telling me what to do. I guess it has been that way all my life. Not understanding then what it was and the reason why it was, but I understand it now, just a by-product of not having a disciplined life and being accountable. I also looked at it in a different aspect as well. God has created us to be kings inferior to no man. That's something to think about. But I realize that there are laws to be subjected to that keep order, so I respect that.

Chapter 1: BUG

The experience that I gained while in the Air Force was great. I was a keypunch operator in the computer room—the only black person in the computer room—it was hard. It was a lot of prejudice in the Air Force. To see a black man in the computer room was kind of strange. I just felt like I was the token black person, amongst my white peers. But soon that experience faded, it just wasn't for me. I got out on an honorable discharge, basically just tired. I didn't want to be a part of that anymore. I received a lot of good training and discipline out of it though. It taught me a lot of things, helped me to grow into being the man that I am today—to be respectful, to guard myself and to keep myself. While in the Air Force I was exposed to a life that was very different than the life that I was going back to. A life of freedom and prosperity, unlike the one I was accustomed to. Coming back home to the projects all I saw was poverty. Generations unaware of the curse that was upon their lives. I saw grandmothers, mothers, daughters and their daughters all in one project. Something has to be done to change the cycle, but what? Today there are over 60 million children worldwide who have been abandoned by their parents, a hundred thousand children every year.

Wisdom Cries: Things to Think About!

Every two seconds, a child becomes an orphan.
Every 14 seconds, a child is orphaned by AIDS.
1,000,000,000 of the world's families live on less than a dollar a day.
90% of all homeless and runaway children are from fatherless homes
85% of all youth sitting in prison grew up in a Fatherless home.
Girls from fatherless homes are 6.6 times more likely to become teenage mothers.

Chapter 2
"Seven"

Wisdom Cries:

"...then you will know the truth and the truth will set you free.
John 8:32 (NCV)

"if the Son therefore shall make you free, ye shall be free indeed.
(John 8:36)

When coming back home, I realized that I had to make some money. The place where we lived was the same scenario, everybody waited once a month to have something. I just couldn't live like that. So, gambling, robbing and stealing became the grind on the streets for me. My father seemed to be alright now as long as he took his medicine, but I still had to watch out for him. My sister became pregnant while I was gone to the Air force and had a baby—a baby girl. I remember how protective I was of her, keeping all the boys away. It seemed as though, as soon as I left—hmm, I want to say that's life but it's not the right kind of life. But, now I'm home and getting back to the things that I was familiar with. My girlfriend, who is now my wife, soon left to attend school at Wichita State University and I was at home, so it made it kind of rough for us. We separated for a minute. During that time I started dating another young lady and my first born son was born out of that relationship. Oh how proud I was, my first son born on the fourth of July, how appropriate?

At this particular time in my life it seemed as though I was lost and couldn't find my way, just wandering. I soon got back with my wife and we really started to date. She became pregnant, soon after, we were married and had a baby girl. It was 1986. I'll never forget September 6, something that I wasn't ready for. Although I loved my wife, as a man I just felt like I was inadequate. I think that's what men fear most about marriage. Not to the point that we're not men, but to the point that we just feel like we can't take care of what's been given to us. It makes us feel like less of a man. Financially, I knew that I wasn't ready without a house or a job—things that bring

My wife was going one direction and I was going another.

stability and security to a relationship. God really wasn't part of my life then either. My wife was going one direction and I was going another but by the grace of God it worked out.

As I see things looking back, my kids were the most important thing to me. Remembering when I was a kid how I did without, man I didn't want my kids to live that way—ever. I just made up in my mind that that was not going to happen. I found myself back in the streets hustling, selling drugs, and basically whatever I could do to make some money. If I couldn't talk you out of it, I stole it and if I couldn't steal it, I took it. But that life led down a road of self-destruction for me. It is by God's grace that I sit here today expounding on my life.

...I was introduced to crack cocaine. The drug that ravished our community and literally the world.

At 24 years old, I was introduced to crack cocaine; the drug that ravished our community and literally the world. The book that I would like to introduce to you by Gary Webb, *Dark Alliances*, explains everything you may have ever wondered about crack cocaine. The effects, the reason why and how it came about. How crack cocaine came to the black community and how it destroyed us. We'll get into that later. I was smoking weed and drinking every now and then, but only for recreational purposes. I didn't really feel like I was strung out or anything like that, and I was never a big drinker. One day though, while hanging with a friend of mine, we were just sitting around mixing this drug called crack in marijuana, smoking it. It really didn't do anything to me, gave me a sense of high for five or ten minutes and went away, which caused me to smoke more and more. I was like man this is a waste of money and a waste of time or so I thought to myself.

Each weekend I found myself going back to it though. And what they call a weekend smoker became an everyday thing for me. I came to understand that I was addicted. All the money that I made working and all the money that I made selling drugs (marijuana) I used to support that habit of crack cocaine. All the things that you've dealt with in your own life with people using this drug, I've been there. From taking T.V.'s and VCR's out of my house, to spending all of my money, even some of my wife's money, to the point I was so ashamed that I left home.

I had gotten to a point in my life where I had no value on my life or anybody else's. I had been robbing, stealing and was pretty much out of control. Around this time everybody started to call me Seven. They said that I was just really lucky. Even when I gambled I always won—certain things that took place were just always in my favor—so this name stuck with me through all of this. The way I looked at it, I never was one to believe in luck because my daddy always taught me that luck was nothing but skill practiced over and over again. During the course of my life I'd been given many names—but never a drug addict. It hurt me to the core of my being. I began to live in dope houses, and soon I began to rob dope houses. I had no understanding about anything. There were times in my life where I should have been dead, over a hundred times or maybe a thousand. Staying up seven to ten days at a time in drug houses, there were times that I would be so high that I could see my heart coming through my chest.

This period of my life was hard. I got with some gentlemen through this dope house that I was about to rob. I went in the house and came to find out that the person who was over the house was like my big brother, he had grown up with me on the block. I remembered him like it was yesterday because I remembered when he was on crack, the first person that I'd really seen on crack. I remember people would talk about him all the time. I'd see him and think, man that's G, he's like my big brother. Every time that I saw him he would ask me for five or ten dollars and if I had it, I'd give it to him despite what was wrong with him. But this day I was at his house getting high in the backroom with some girls, I'll never forget it. They said here comes G-money and all the girls ran out the room and the house. Well it's more dope for me, I thought to myself. Hearing everyone coming back to the room, he said, "Bug, is that you?" "Yea, what's up?" I said. That relationship kept me in that environment for months. I got real close to him and began to sell drugs in numerous dope houses.

It's a life that I really don't want to exploit or speak on because it caused so much havoc in our neighborhoods and our community. I don't think we've recovered from it yet. So in this chapter I don't want to glamorize this way of life. All I know is while sharing this with you I should be dead today. Looking back on how God spared my life over and over again after I've robbed people and seen them a week later. It's like the person didn't know or remember who I was. He even kept bullets from hitting me and many other things. It's nothing but His grace that I'm alive today.

I remember that I robbed a little guy who was on the corner selling drugs; he had a whole Ziploc bag full of crack cocaine. It was a girl that came up on me looking to buy some drugs on credit. I told her I didn't have any right now I'm just chilling and told her that the guy across the street had some. I gave her $20 and she ran across the street. While over there, the little guy talked so bad to her that she started cussing and what not. I asked her what was wrong and she began telling me what happened. I went over to talk to the young man and he just talked real crazy to me. I made up in my mind that as soon as it got dark, I was going to rob him. Later as I walked back across the street towards him, I told him to let me look at some of his drugs. He was selling crack packaged. I used to carry this glocc 9mm pistol. As soon as he looked down, I put it to his head and said, "break yourself!" He dropped the bag, trying to run I grabbed him by the shirt and took all his jewelry and his little money. He had about two or three thousand dollars and a bag full of dope. I kicked him in the butt and told him to get on, so he took off running.

Now I'm walking back across the street to a guy who's working on my car. He tells me that it won't be finished until tomorrow, so me and a friend of mine named Buck are walking down 33rd and Indiana towards Central High School in Kansas City, MO. We see a blue Cadillac coming down the street with a real loud muffler hanging off of the car. As soon as he got near us, he pulled over on the side of the street up on the curb. A man pulled out a shot gun, pointed it at us and said, "Man you the guy that robbed my little brother." "That's not me you got the wrong person," I replied. "Nah that's you, he said you had on overalls." All of a sudden the police are coming from around the corner of Linwood to Indiana, hitting the sirens, making a U-turn in the middle of the street— all the while I'm thinking he's about to get this guy for being all up on the curb. But he doesn't, he goes in the opposite direction which gave us time to run. As my friend and I started to run you could hear the buckshots hitting the trees. It happened so fast and all I know is that I was in between a car and curb on the next block on Bales almost scared to death. I sat there for five minutes in between this car and the curb trembling, when I hear the car coming again. I could tell based on the sound of the muffler. I'm thinking to myself, but I don't know what to do. As the car goes by I realize that I have this pistol. Raising up, running to the bushes my plan was to wait for him to come back around and give him the business. Luckily, or by the grace of God I should say, he didn't come back around. I looked at that

> *I was in the world and I lived how the world lived.*

situation and how God spared me even in that, I saw my life flash before my eyes.

I've had many reoccurring nightmares about things I've done wrong. I know God has delivered me from them and I know that the devil has tried to bring them to my remembrance to keep me in condemnation. I was in the world and I lived how the world lived. I'll never forget being in dope houses and the way that life is. I wish that on nobody. During this time we had four dope houses that were open 24 hours a day. It was a life that you get caught up in and before you know it, you're shipwrecked. God had warned me, while I was selling drugs of the destruction that lied ahead if I stayed on that path. as I look back at the thing that had me in bondage, I didn't take heed and I felt that I had gone from bad to worse because I began to sell the same thing that had me in bondage, to my own people and to other people as well. It seemed like that drug was targeted towards our culture, it ravished our black community.

I couldn't understand why it was so. We didn't have any factories, we didn't have any planes. I remember back in the day cocaine was a rich man's drug, but it found its way into the ghettoes of our communities. I couldn't understand that. Again we have no planes or factories to manufacture and distribute drugs or guns. It seems like all the guns in the world have been in the black neighborhoods. Where I live in Kansas City, MO., I think there's a gun show every month or two and they wonder where the young black males get guns. They can't go in the store and buy one over the counter. You have to have a license and most of them are too young. I remember when I was in the dope house, I had 20 guns under my mattress and

I couldn't shoot but one or two of them. How did they all get into my neighborhood? It's certainly not enough money in the city for everybody to have the kinds of guns that they have, back when I was selling drugs and not to mention the guns they have now out in our communities.

At this time God's hand was still on my life. He protected me from sudden death numerous times. His warning came to me one day. A friend of mine that I grew up with had come over to the dope house. I was upstairs in my room when they called me down and said, "Pete somebody wants to see you downstairs." I look around the corner and they tell me it's a guy who was driving a Mercedes Benz, so I'm thinking to myself he must have some money. That was my cue. So I thought, "I'll go downstairs." When I get down there I looked around the corner and noticed that it's a gentleman named Kenny who I grew up with. Before I could pull my head back he saw me and said, "Bug, let me talk to you." He was the only person besides "G" who knew me by that name. We had all grown up together. As he said that, I came on downstairs, he said, "I got something that I have to tell you and I can't leave until I do." I went out on the porch and saw his car in the driveway. I said, "Man you can't leave your car in front of the driveway like that, this is a dope house." His wife and kids were in there. He was just coming back from church. He said, "The Holy Ghost told me to come over here and tell you that you need to get out this house because something bad is going to happen." So I'm like, "Oh man Kenny, man don't come over here trying to burn bread on me;" and I'm going on and on but he was so adamant that he wouldn't leave unless I left with him. I told him that I couldn't leave these guns and drugs with these gentlemen, because they would mess my stuff up. He told me that I could put it in the trunk and he would take me all the way home.

We were on 29th and Brooklyn and I stayed on 75th Terrace. We rode down Prospect that night at 1:30 or 2 in the morning—probably one of the wrong streets to drive down late at night. The police patrol that street all night. But that night we made it to my house safe and sound. I looked through the window of my door and saw my wife sitting on the couch looking like she was crying. I got through the door and she jumped on me saying she loved me and she was glad I was home and this and that. I really didn't understand what was going on

Chapter 2: Seven

and why I was almost crying. That was a Sunday night. I stayed home Monday and Tuesday, but that Wednesday I had to go down to the dope house to get my money that I had left. Something was wrong with my car; it wasn't running so I asked my wife to let me use the van. We had bought a new Chevy Lumina. She began to argue with me, "No, if you leave, you're not coming back." Now that I think about it, I didn't come back. Anyways, she ended up hiding the keys from me, I got mad, and walked to the liquor store. I figured just to get away from the house. It was like a voice came out of the sky and said, "You can ride the metro bus down there." I'm looking around thinking somebody was on a porch or something talking to me but I didn't see anybody. So when I get up to the corner the bus is sitting right there on the corner. I said to myself, "I can ride the bus down here right quick." I tell the man on the bus, "hold it, hold it," He says, "nah man take your time, I'm waiting on you." It was kind of strange how everything was going. I ran into the store and got some beer and some cigarettes and came back and got on the bus. Still thinking about what Kenny had been telling me, I had intended to come back home in a couple of hours. But two hours turned into four and four hours turned into six. I saw G and I told him, "Man come and get me around 10 so I can go home. I don't want to stay down here in this house." He said "alright" but he never came. I ended up going down to a hotel because it was the beginning of the month and during that time that's when the money was plentiful. So I went down there selling drugs, I just didn't want to be in that house—how ironic.

I came back the next morning. Everything was going on. The house was still rolling as before. Like I said, it was the beginning of the month and money was everywhere. During the course of the day a guy was in the house high on PCP. He began to shoot firecrackers in the house. They called me downstairs and said, "Man there's a guy down here that's high and tripping." The person that they happened to be talking about was "G's" cousin. I told him, "Man you can't do that in here, the police will come and think we're shooting in the house or something." "Man this is my cousin's house and I can do what I want to do." He replied. Ok—you not gone do it in here.

During this time in my life I was cussing a lot and really didn't have a lot of understanding or tolerance for foolishness.

Chapter 2: Seven

So I said, "Alright man, whatever you say." He followed me upstairs and was still talking. Based on respect for his cousin I really didn't want to give him the business. The thing is, he was talking about lighting a firecracker or bottle rocket and throwing it in my room. I told him, "Man if you light anything in here I'm going to shoot you." About an hour before this I had bought a 25 automatic out of a box—brand new pistol. I was outside shooting it because it sounded like firecrackers. The guy was steady talking. I had my pistol on a TV tray and I was cutting up drugs on the tray. There was a girl on my bed and another guy in my room. The girl screamed and said, "He's lighting it, he's lighting it!" He lit a bottle rocket in my room. I picked up the pistol, pointed it at him and pulled the trigger. The gun didn't work—but I knew it worked because I had just been outside shooting it. All the bullets were in it but it wasn't working then. The guy took off running. I reached under my mattress, grabbed another gun, a 9mm—I *knew* this worked. I ran downstairs and heard him ask somebody for a gun. In the ruckus of it I'm trying to shoot him and hit him at the same time with the pistol. They put him out of the house.

At this point I'm really mad. I went out on the back deck of the house. I was sitting there with my 9mm, a shotgun, and my 25 automatic. I said, "if he comes back, I'm gonna give him the business." I was sitting there and five minutes later I heard a whole lot of noise and chaos. I saw people running past me on the side of the house. I got up and looked on the side and saw two police officers kick in vans—the "DEA" and the "Tobacco and Firearms." They came busting in the house and I'm started throwing everything under the deck, drugs, guns everything—before I could get up on the ledge to jump over into a vacant lot to go through an alley

...This one cloud came right over this house and it started sprinkling on me as they put the handcuffs on me. I just believe even God cried at that moment.

in the back, 20 police officers came from the back yard of the other side of the block pointing guns at me. I heard the guns clicking, "Get down, get down!" "Don't shoot, don't shoot!" I said. I lay down on the deck and I'll never forget it just like it was yesterday. It was a beautiful sunny day, not a cloud in the sky but, at this moment, this one cloud came right over this house and it started sprinkling on me as they put the handcuffs on me. I just believe even God cried at that moment. But the thing about it was it was a choice that I made. It was my fault. I blamed nobody else. I look back and think that if I had shot that gentleman or if he had shot me, I wouldn't be here right now. I just really thank God for his grace and his mercy. With all of the things that I've been through, even with my addiction that almost tore up my family. But by the grace of God as well as having a praying wife who travailed in birth till Christ was formed in me I prevailed. She wouldn't let the devil have me. I thank God for her. She is an extraordinary woman built to last, tough as nails, yet soft as cotton. She's been my helpmate truly in this life—you'll hear more about her a little later.

Wisdom Cries: Things to Think About

Statistics on Addiction

19.5 million people over the age of 12 use illegal drugs in the U.S.
19,000 deaths occur from drug addiction a year
In federal court today, low level crack dealers and first-time offenders sentenced for

Trafficking of crack cocaine receive an average sentence of 10 years and 6 months

Chapter 3
"Deacon"

Wisdom cries:

> *For we will surely die and become like water spilt on the ground which cannot be gathered up again if God does not take away a life, but He devises means so that his banished ones are not expelled from Him.*
>
> **2 Samuel 14:14 (NKJV)**

Black males continue to be incarcerated at an extraordinary rate. Black males make up 35.4% of the jail and prison population even though they make up less than 10% of the overall U.S. population. More than 60% of people in prison are now racial and ethnic minorities. For black men in their 20s, one in every eight is in prison or jail on any given day.

Man where have they got me at now? Maybe I'll get out on a 20-hour investigation. That's when they come in there and ask you all these questions and you say that you don't know "nothing"—then they let you go after 20 hours of keeping you in jail. That's what usually happens when they come and kick in the dope houses. Unless you are an operation 100, that's when they cut all the lights off on the block because they can't get inside the dope house. This life is crazy. I see some of the guys that were in the dope house with me. Some of them are missing, some are still here. They call my name. I'm thinking I'm about to be released. They say the marshals are coming to get you. I'm like marshal who? Little did I know that they were taking me across the street to the federal building where I met all of my co-defendants (or all of the guys who were on my case).

Man I didn't know what to think. I began to be afraid, but not scared. I figured they were just going to play with us and then let us go, calling us out one at a time to see what we knew. They called my name and asked me did I know such and such or did I know about this or that. I didn't know anything. They said that I was facing 40 years in prison. I just laughed. Man you got to be kidding, I'm saying to myself. I haven't done anything to deserve 40 years. They threw a stack of pictures on the table. "So this is not you? This is not_____, "I don't know who that is. It's not me." "That's alright." They said. "We got something for you." They sent me back to my cell. Here comes a guard bringing me an indictment, the United States of America vs. unidentified black male. Until they fingerprinted me, I thought that they were unsure of who I was since on my indictment stated unidentified male. Then I came to understand after that night that they knew all about me. As I was facing this indictment, they kept stressing this 40 years. I'm telling

Going in you have to basically give up all of your rights— the clothes you wore, sometimes even your mannerism.

you, my wife and those close to me, came to grips with the fact that I might need a little help and there wasn't anything that they could do. My wife began to pray—as always.

All I felt was bitter and alone. Not understanding, feeling like this was a dream, but man this is reality. The next thing I knew, I was in Leavenworth penitentiary. Afraid but never scared. But this place would nearly change my mind about that thought. Going in you had to basically give up all of your rights—the clothes you wore, sometimes even your mannerism. After that, they take you through a metal detector, in some places an x-ray machine, removing all of your clothes stripping you naked, checking in every crevice of your body; the most humiliating thing that I've ever seen or experienced. I couldn't understand this. This is inhumane I thought, as they were giving me an orange jumpsuit. Man this is a weird feeling. Thinking about all of the stories that I heard about jail; how it was and how men were getting raped and all the things that you see on TV. But nothing could compare to this right here—nothing at all.

As I step onto the yard through an opening in the hallway, basically a sliding door comes down and opens to a ramp, which leads to what convicts call "the yard." Looking like a playground for grownups, it has a giant track with basketball goals and numerous other physical things to do. My first day on the yard a new arrival, realizing the life I once lived no longer exists. **Fifteen years**!—how could I do this? Standing there on the ramp gazing at the scenery there's about 500 men on this yard with a population of 2500. "Man," where have they got me? Someone shouted my name; I thought to myself, "who knows me here?" One of my co-defendants, I didn't know he was here. As we began to talk, a man ran up the ramp with a stocking over his face drew back and stabbed a black man in the back three times as he hollered with each thrust. It was about 20 men standing there, we all scattered like roaches when you turn the lights on, while the man with the mask took off back into the building. This is crazy and this is only my third day here.

As time went on I began to study the law and understand that they couldn't give me 40 years. But I was facing almost 25 for the things that they had charged me with. I knew I couldn't go to trial—two of my co-defendants began to tell—what we call now, snitching. That left the rest of us in quite a tight situation. They came with deals and offers of 20 or 25 years. I declined, because I understood that they didn't have all the things that they said. But when we went to our evidentiary hearing it really changed our minds about the decision that we would make. Walking in a court room chained up, all of us, looking at a table maybe 10 feet long with about 50 guns on the table—two to three keys of crack, 7 oz. or so of crack, and boxes of food stamps and money. As soon as we saw that we knew that we were guilty. What we didn't know was that all this time there was three people that had already told. As soon as we saw this reality began to sink in. We were in jail and quite possibly not getting out. As always they appoint you a court-appointed lawyer if you don't have the money to pay for one. From my experience, even if you had money it would be a waste of

We were in jail and quite possibly not getting out.

time based on the feds conviction rates of about 99.9% based on the help of snitches. Let me clarify that I'm not saying that in malice or bitterness because I don't know what another man goes through in the situation he might be facing. My father always told me, to "handle your weight." So I took it to mean that the things that you do, be responsible for.

Some things that I discuss may be somewhat graphic. Through my experiences in prison, those who told or those we called snitches, were either checked in the hole, stabbed up or found dead somewhere. They were really hard on those who told. Something I came to understand while in prison is that we found out who told before the people on the streets did. It's like a world inside of a world. When you come inside that world you're a part of that world. You can't live outside that world and live on the streets and be in prison—you can't do it. I've seen men drive themselves crazy. Even those who have told on people and have tried to live amongst their peers it's hard for them. Every day they have to worry about someone else finding out that they did someone wrong.

As I look back, life in the beginning of my incarceration was only bitterness. I fought all the time and went back and forth to the hole. I lost a lot of my good time going to the hole. The hole is the place where they send you when you're a rebellious inmate that contains a concrete slab, a sink and a toilet stool made out of steel all connected together in your room. The strange thing about it was I had such peace in there, because I didn't want to be in or around that environment. It was crazy every day. All I thought about was my wife and my children. Not wanting to, but somehow I was compelled to. My youngest daughter was being born at this time. My kids were my world. You know in prison your wife is not so secure—or your woman or your lady. I've seen guys lose their wives the first week, or the first month or the first year. Asking or expecting someone to wait for you on the other side of a prison sentence is hard. It takes an extraordinary woman—a woman of God I should say—cause only God could keep you together. I used to think about guys whose women had left them. I had a conversation with one guy. I said "well, where did you meet her?" He replied that he met her in the club. I thought to myself you were doing all of this stuff for her and you met her in the club. Now that you're gone where do you think she's going to gravitate towards? Reality kind of hit him in the face along with a letter that she had written saying that she was leaving. It keeps your defenses up because you don't want to be vulnerable.

I remember having a conversation with my wife about whether she would stay or not. She said that she would, but I wasn't convinced, after hearing all of the stories when I got to prison about another man being around your kids or being in your house. That bothered me. That was something that I never wanted, someone around my kids. It was just that I became naturally suspicious. I remembered how it was when I was little—having strange people around not knowing who they were and what they were capable of. I thank God that even while I was little that I was never molested—my brother or my sister either. We were never sexually abused. Just physically with the whooping's or beatings that my mother would give us. But through all the things in life, nothing compared to this right here.

Everything that you have and everything that you love is taken from you and only God knows when you'll get it back. You're alone and when you come to this place you actually understand what alone truly means.

...Life in prison is monotonous. It's a routine over and over again. The only thing that changes is life and death.

Nothing is safe. Nothing is secure. Depending on the penitentiary that you're in you have to watch everything that you do and everybody. As I began to indulge in prison life, it became monotonous. It's a routine over and over again. The only thing that changes is life and death. No matter where you're at time is going by, that's the one thing you have to always remember— they can't stop time.

Later I found myself in the Midwest at a prison hospital where inmates like myself begin to take care of those inmates who are sick or those in need. This is a high security level place with people from the ADX—those who have been under 24 hour lock down and have now come to this place and are free in some aspects to even walk around. You have every level from the ADX to the high to medium to even low. Those are the degrees of your level of crime or violence. In this place everybody was the same, everybody wore the same clothes, the same shoes, everybody could only spend the same amount of money. They had a place called commissary where you bought the extra stuff that they didn't have in your chow hall or wherever you ate at every day.

Looking back at this place, man it was graphic. Being that it was a hospital you saw guys walking around with no legs, no arms, tubes sticking out of their necks and cancer eating up their face. Then you have a part of this place called "ten" building. Where the mentally unstable are in a sense warehoused—probably a thousand inmates who have either lost their mind through the pressures of life, through drugs, doing time, or were faking trying to beat their case and started taking medicine. The medicine then started to mess them up. This place is unreal, like no other. It makes you thankful that you have your health—not to mention that you're just alive. I worked on a floor called 3-2. As soon as you get off the elevator you can smell death on the floor. It was a terminally ill ward where guys were dying from AIDs, cancer, tuberculosis, those who were paraplegics who couldn't move from the waist or the neck down—I worked at this place for maybe two years. In the first year I saw almost 25 people—inmates, die from disease. At times some things were abnormal. It was like they were experimenting on them. One would be alright one day and the next he would be dead. As a nursing attendant it was my job to basically take care of those who couldn't take care of themselves, from writing letters to family members, giving baths, shopping for them and more. It was a hard job but I was thankful. Not so much for just being alive but more so because I wasn't like them. This right here was probably the hardest part of my life.

The first two years of my incarceration, I spent probably 16-18 months in the hole from fighting. When I was out that's when I worked on 3-2 ward. Now that I look back I was only hurting myself. I lost a lot of good time during that time in my life. The only real thing that was a blessing in my life was that I had an encounter with Jesus in the hole. I had got in trouble for something and although my wife would pray and preach to me when I talked to her on the phone I was still in "that place." A lot of things took place in that room that day. I had gone to the hole so many times that they had given me my own room. "Just send him on down to his room," they'd say. This last time that I went I asked for a Bible. I came to a place where I really just got tired and was at my wit's end. I was bitter; I was angry, mostly angry with God. I knew that Him being God that he knew this was going to happen to me. That was my resolve or my reasoning and he allowed it to happen. With all the stuff that my wife was preaching about he allowed this to happen.

I was bitter; I was angry and mostly angry with God.

So I blamed Him and it caused me to be real bitter. This day though, my experience with God was different. It was like no other day. I prayed that day and I asked God, if it works for everybody else—serving You—let it work for me. It was just that simple. At that moment, God seemed to in a sense enter the cell. Before my eyes I began to see all the things that I had done wrong. At that moment I truly felt the weight of sin. God allowed me to see what sin was really like; what doing wrong was all about and how much

I had an encounter with God and it was different than all the things I had experienced in life.

harm it causes. I remember just balling up in a fetal position and crying like a baby uncontrollably. In prison you don't let men see you cry. For some reason although I wasn't around any men at this time it really didn't make a difference. I had an encounter with God and it was different than all the things I had experienced in life.

I remember meeting a man right before I came to prison named Dr. Steve Houpe, my sister-in-law would always talk about him to my wife. I would kind of blow it off like yea, yea, yea—to me all preachers were the same. Anyway my wife started going to this church on 63rd street. At this time in my life I was still selling drugs, getting high, carrying guns and all kinds of stuff. Every time she would come home from church she would always talk, about "Pastor this and Pastor that." In my heart as a man I'm beginning to be almost envious thinking, "who is this Pastor? He's gone make me bust a cap in Him?!" And that was my thought process back then. But curiosity got the best of me. Just to see who he was because my wife was around and listening to him, I went to church one Sunday. It seemed like he was only preaching to me. I looked at my wife, I'm mad, 38 hot, thinking that she had told this man all of my business, but God dealt with me that day through the Holy Ghost. I remember a lady asking did anyone want to receive the Holy Ghost. I was out on bond facing 15 years. I had already taken my plea and knew how much time I would get but didn't want to do it. At this moment something compelled me to get up out of the seat. In myself it was not me. This lady laid hands on me to receive the Holy Spirit and at that moment I was filled. My wife and other people tell me stories about it how I was dancing uncontrollably and other things but I couldn't remember one thing. I just knew that day, that something was different and that something was different about this man of God.

Chapter 3: Deacon

That encounter although it was great couldn't compare to this one I was having in the hole. When I say that, I'm not taking for granted that which had happened prior, I just believe that God was working in me then to get me to this point where I was now; on my face balled up like a baby. I came out of the hole a different man—a different person. God delivered me from a lot of things that day, from drugs, from malice, from hatred.

I understood that I had to begin to change the way that I thought about things. God in his brilliance and his mercy brought a man all the way from South America named Raphael Jackman from Guyana, Georgetown to disciple me. I met him as I moved into a new building which they called 9 building. This gentleman had the brightest smile and that's all he did was smile. Somehow God intertwined us together and I followed him as he followed Christ. Every time that you were around him you could feel the anointing on him. At that time I didn't know what the anointing was but I knew that something was different about him. He didn't watch a lot of TV; as a matter of fact he didn't watch any TV at all. He might have watched a soccer game every now and then because he loved soccer. He taught me all he knew about the Bible and he blessed me tremendously. I followed him in the things of God. But I was bitter—or rather, it was too much weight for me to carry at that time in my life. It was a strict regimen, I didn't watch TV, I stopped playing basketball—I stopped doing the things that I loved doing that were a part of my life, and my flesh cried out. So I had a conversation with him one day and he said, "It took me five years to get like this, through disciplining myself and reading and understanding the Word of God—you can't be me you have to be you." When he shared that with me it was like a boulder had lifted up off of my shoulders and I came to understand that God made me, as an individual and that I could only be me and not anyone else. Raphael truly blessed me and if he's reading this book, wherever he's at I pray that he would find me just so that I could bless him from my heart. He meant a lot to me and he helped to keep me in my time of need by imparting the Word of God to me.

As a result of that relationship God was able to impart wisdom to me because I began to study and seek his face. They came to ask me if I would go and teach Bible Study on Saturdays to the inmates and I agreed.

Chapter 3: Deacon

God was doing some extraordinary things in my life. These were things that people who knew me on the streets knew wasn't me. They knew that God had done something for me. Every time they saw me I was carrying my Bible. I remember a guy asked me, "Why are you always carrying that Bible around all the time?" I told him that I had to. It was mandatory for me to do this because it was the only thing that kept my mind and kept me from slipping away, from being angry, from not having patience things that would get me back in trouble.

For five years straight I read and walked around with that Bible. I went to church five or six days out of the week, every day of the week for any kind of function worshipping God or seeking Jesus. For a

For a time in my life that was seemingly so low, God blessed me tremendously and gave me so much.

time in my life that was seemingly so low, God blessed me tremendously and gave me so much. As I helped others he helped me. He blessed my wife and my children to have the best things in life. While I was incarcerated for all the 16 years that I was there, God blessed them to have all their needs met, they never wanted for anything other than me.

It took a while for me to get established and rooted because I was in a place where they didn't care whether you were a Christian or whatever you were, whether you loved God or served Him. I believe that it was the devil's playground based on the principalities that were over every prison that I had been to. There's a sense of death in every prison that you go to. There's malice, there's hatred, there's anger. These spirits populate most prisons although there are Christians and men of God who pray always without ceasing; these places exist and are real. The only way that you can walk through this is with God's hand on your life, especially if you're serving a lot of time. God began to change some things in my life even in the relationship with my wife. It seemed to be an about face.

I remember the first year that I tried to divorce my wife and waiting the third year and the fifth year—how stupid of me. But during that time based on my insecurities and my lack of loving myself I tried to push her away. She wouldn't have it though. It was her belief in God that I couldn't really understand at the time. But I understand it now. I couldn't understand how a woman could love a man—well not so much even love a man—but love God so much that she would love a man the way that God had called her to. I say a lot of things about her and really don't give her the credit she's due. I just want to say in this book that I thank her for blessing me as a helpmate. I thank her for raising my children in the admonition of the Lord as well as myself. I thank her most for loving God because without her there's no telling where I would be. I have to admit as a man there are some

When everybody else left, friends, family, when they departed, (my wife) stood there, she stood strong.

areas that I probably could have endured without her, but God gave me his best and he knew that I needed her. When everybody else left, friends, family, when they departed, my wife stood there, she stood strong. Even when I tried to get rid of her she stood there. I'm indebted to her and I love her not because of what she's done or what she did by staying and just trusting God but I love her because of who she is. She's a genuine person, has always been on the straight and narrow. When I was living in the world, she was always facing towards God above all else. Honestly, man I remember when we first got married, we went to the grocery store and they gave her 19 cents over and she was counting on our way home saying that she had to take the money back they gave me too much and the devil isn't going to steal anything from me and all this. And I'm thinking, "Girl we're not going all the way back to the store over 19 cents." "Well you can take me home and I'll drive back on my own" she said. So just wanting to protect her I took her back to the store so she could give the 19 cents back. Looking at her at that time I couldn't understand, I mean what kind of woman is this. But now I see clearly—at first I was looking through a glass darkly.

Just with her as I said before praying me through, I tell my brothers out there if you have a good wife, a good woman, the Bible says that a man that findeth a wife finds a good thing and obtaineth favor from the Lord (**Proverbs 18:22**). Man don't you get rid of her, don't you run her away. I understand being in jail and not wanting to be close to anybody based on the fear of not being hurt but God has a special person for you. I just pray that when she reads this book that she'll be blessed because she's blessed me. She's always been there for me and stood by my side even when I was wrong and so I love her with all of my heart and all of my being. There's nothing that I won't do for her, not based only on what she has done but because I love her for the woman that she is.

So as life began to change on the inside, God began to do some miraculous things. He opened the door for me to go over into this place called 10 building, which is another part of the prison I was in, to teach the Bible to those who were mentally unstable. Some of the things I read in the Bible couldn't compare to the things that I saw over in this place, for example, the two men in the tombs in (Matthew 8:28-34) or Legion. I've literally seen these spirits on men in prison. Not only in this place, but in numerous other prisons, these men are debased and perverted, who take advantage of young boys sent to prison through extortion, rape, and mind control. Imagine your son or any young boy sent to prison at 15, 16, 17 or 18 years of age, put in a two man cell with a man that's been down 20 years, with a life sentence who would rather have a man than a woman. If no one comes to his rescue he will be raped, and if you send any money it will be taken through extortion, and if he has no money coming in, he will be pimped out (passed around to other convicts) for cigarettes and money. As you're reading this book you're probably thinking that somebody would have to kill you before they rape you. Listen, you're no match for a man who's been working out, on "swole," muscles everywhere, and you come in weighing a buck-o-five. Remember there are no guns in this place; you can't shoot your way out. So if you can't fight or maybe you can, but now there are two men instead of one—what are you going to do? To the reader, these things happened at every prison. If a man's mind isn't strong enough it will sink to its lowest depths after doing decades of time. This is what is referred to as being "institutionalized!" God, help us! So getting back to the story, this was a great opportunity for me to help, but as I entered this place, man there's something about it, strange, men walking around like zombies, doped up on medication. "God be with me," I'd always say as I walked the halls to the room prepared for Bible Study.

Chapter 3: Deacon

Most men came because of curiosity, some looking for God. Either way, I was eager to share the wisdom of God. But that third week made me almost reconsider coming over to this place. I remember it like it was yesterday. I had about twelve guys that I was teaching in the class, all of a sudden one of the men crawled onto the table, it was so fast it was as if he jumped from a seated position, growling he said, "I'm the devil, get out." The hair stood up on my head and I was bald headed.

...One of the men crawled onto the table, it was so fast it was as if he jumped from a seated position, growling he said, "I'm the devil, get out."

Fear rushed in like a flood, but something rose up within me and I shouted, "Sit down in Jesus' name and be quiet!" That's when I truly knew the power in that name. He crawled back in the seat so fast, at attention and quiet, but the strangest thing was, I never saw him again and I was over there for a year or so teaching.

It's sad; I've seen men who have literally lost their minds who they couldn't allow out in population. They are behind big steel doors that have a big wheel and a chuckhole to slide their food through because they can't have any human contact. I've seen men on suicide watch. I saw a man stick a pencil up his penis running around the room laughing saying that he was the devil. I've seen men cut their wrists and smear blood all over walls and still live not understanding why they would do things of this sort.

In this place every dorm was lettered A, B, C, D and so on with 200 inmates probably in each. They went all the way back to G or H and the further they went back the worse off they were. They kept me in the front where the guys were less aggressive and manageable in a sense. As a barber in prison I was able to go back there and cut hair. I cut some men's hair that had been in one room for 15-20 years. One guy they brought out in a Hannibal Lecter chair with a helmet on and faceguard. It kind of startled me at first but he was all chained down and locked up and had about 10 guards around him. They took the helmet off and his hair was all matted and wild. As I looked at him in the eyes he seemed like a normal individual with the mouth guard over him he didn't say anything. I asked him how he wanted his hair cut, he just shrugged his shoulders. As I began to cut his hair from the front they told me I couldn't do that and that I had to cut it from the back—I'm thinking how can this man get up out of this chair with all of these chains and straps on him. But anyway, I cut his hair; they put the helmet back on him and wheeled him back out of there. Come to find out this man had killed three guards and maybe a couple of prisoners. There was no telling what he had done while he was on the streets if he did all of that in jail.

Every day that you woke up in this place you had to be conscious of where you were at, at all times. There was always somebody watching you so you had to be watchful. This place was like no other and I'm talking about prison. But over here where I taught this class in 10 building, these guys are taken advantage of amongst themselves, by the police or by doctors. Some of them are given P-numbers based on how bad they are. In some cases some of them may have done 20 years before they even got sentenced or before they were able to stand trial and be cognizant of what's going on but they've already done 25 or 30 years inside this place. When you start seeing things like this it could really bother you. And what made it so bad is if you were a convict like me and you decided to buck or act slightly out of control, in some prisons they would put you over there. They had a hole over in this place that you just didn't want to be in. Screaming and hollering all day in this place and the further back you went the worse off it was. Men were getting raped daily.

I learned a lot about my father and about the things that he was going through dealing with schizophrenia from being over there. Although God did a great work for me and in me in that place there is so much more that is needed. I just want to thank Ted Green who was part of the prison ministry and came in and talked to the brothers on Wednesday nights and at times went with me over to 10 building on those Thursday evenings. I want to thank Ted for just volunteering and if he's reading this, thank you Ted, I love you man.

Now, getting back to the incarceration, some things that you hear like I said before, may be graphic. For the purpose of not dragging the story on, because 16 years is a long time and there is a lot that I could write about but right now those things that were impactful to my life are the things that I will share with you.

As I stated before one of the main reasons for me writing this book I believe is to tell people don't come here. This is real. Don't go to prison. It is designed for you systematically, especially for my Black and Latino brothers, to be incarcerated. Due to the harsh new sentencing guidelines such as, the three strikes you're out law. A number of young black and Hispanic men are likely to be in prison for life under the scenarios for which they are guilty for little more than a history of untreated addictions and several prior drug related offenses. When you look at certain things like this, if we don't reach them before this happens, the posterity that we talk about saving won't exist.

...Blacks only account for 12% of the U.S. population but 44% of all prisoners in the U.S. are black.

I was looking at some of the statistics the other day, such as blacks only account for 12% of the U.S. population, but 44% of all prisoners in the U.S. are black. During my incarceration I couldn't understand why everywhere I went there were only Latino and Black brothers even in the place where I just described. It seemed like a conspiracy. Just like I told you before, read the book by Gary Webb called, *"Dark Alliances."* It will bless you and help you to understand why our black inner city youth and our Latino brothers are being targeted. The powers that be may say they aren't, but based upon the war on drugs, the majority and the minority they are the only two races that are populating probably 60% of most prisons right now (and I could of course go deeper but I won't due to the things that I want to cover in this book).

God used me to bless a lot of brothers and his hand was on my life. After so many years in one place they start to move you around. Basically it's a mandatory thing based on security so I found myself going through transit ready to move. Going over to a holding center to get on a plane—usually the holding center in Oklahoma. You stay there and it's the same routine everywhere you go. You get butt-naked they strip search you, take all your clothes off, they look all in the crack of your butt, in your mouth, your ears, all of that—everywhere you go when you're getting transported to another place this transition happens. When you get to the place that you're going to the same things happen again. The thing that would scare me—and like I said I would be afraid but not scared—was getting on a plane shackled hand and foot with a black box on your wrist preventing you from any type of escape. The key was if the plane crashed who was going to save us? That right there, in and of itself made you just want to think and say hmm. Even right now I have a thing about getting on planes. I seem to get nervous and being that I had gone to six different prisons I was on the plane a lot. Some people say that it was a bad thing; to me it was a good thing because it broke up my time.

I began to experience different things in life just doing time. I went to some of the worst penitentiaries. Even in my state of serving God I wasn't perfect and in jail like I said before it's a world inside a world so you have to make your world work. I found myself up on a hill in Florence, Colorado, which they call gladiator school and it was the worse of the worse they say. They had a camp, a medium security, a penitentiary and an ADX all on the same hill. So if you messed up in one you went on to the next higher one. As I said before the ADX is 24 hour lock down underground, you see no day light. Everything that you read, every contact that you have comes up on a screen, even your mail; if you want to work out they wheel a metal fence to the door of your room probably 4 x 6 feet and that's your rec. You come out of the cage and run up and down that's as far as you go. That's any ADX, if you mess up in the penitentiary that's where they send you, if you mess up in the medium they send you to the penitentiary. They have different levels and at every level there is a new devil.

You have to understand that there are those in prison who prey on the weak and in this place there are no exceptions. Just like when I was in Leavenworth there would be men who'd rather have a man than a woman even if they had a real live woman standing in front of them. We had a term where we called those who preyed on new arrivals based on trying to make men into women "booty-bandits"—and there are other terms that I could use but only those in prison would understand. There are homosexuals walking around in prison. Some have breast, some have long hair and some look more like women than women do. In this environment that we were in these men were worth a lot of money. Whoever owned one or was trading one of them usually had everything going on and had enough money to do the things that he needed to do in prison. Now those who are entering prison, those who have told on somebody and those who have female tendencies, and by the way should I say—you should have no female tendencies if you don't want to be treated like a female. In prison men are naturally drawn to anything soft. If you come in with anything soft about you there will be someone waiting to test your manhood. Based on who you are and who you may know that may not take place, but if you are in a place

There are men having sex with men on a regular basis in prison.

where it's just you or you may have burned all your bridges no one can help you then.

As I said before, this is one of the purposes for me writing this book, to keep as many of my brothers; I don't care whether you're black, brown, green, or orange, to keep you from this place. Rape goes on here all the time and I'm not going to sugar coat it. There are men having sex with men on a regular basis in prison. If you don't want to be one of those men don't come to this place unless you can hold your own. You have to remember that you're checking all your guns and everything in RD. When you come you don't have a gun to shoot across the street so if you can't fight I'm just going to be frank with you you're going to be somebody's woman. Based on what you know or what you don't know mind your business. In this place right here sometimes people try to mind it for you so you have to stand on what you believe in.

Me myself, as a Christian as I began to do time I was one of those persons who wanted to go home and see my wife and kids so I wasn't going to allow anyone to hurt me. That was my whole objective in hurting you.

> *You can't allow people to say certain things or get away with certain things in that environment because if you do someone else will try and take advantage of you.*

Based on however I was living and how I was serving the Lord if you crossed that certain line I had to make you aware that you had crossed the line. In prison it's just that way. You can't allow people to say certain things or get away with certain things in that environment because if you do someone else will try and take advantage of you. As I said before you have to be aware of all your surroundings.

I was awakened one morning to the sounds of loud cussing, two white men arguing, one younger than the other. Rising up out of my bed, they began to fight and since we were in a dorm like room I took a ring-side seat. The younger white man who seemed to be physically stronger, punching the other man in the face, drawing way back connecting with each punch, until he knocked the older man into his cube where he slept. He was lying on top of his desk, dazed and bleeding from his face, but he couldn't tell where the blood was coming from. All the while the younger one walking away with his back turned, cussing talking about how he put it on my man. All of sudden the older gentleman began to rumble through his desk, dazed he rushed at the youngster, wind milling like a girl, or the way girls used to fight. He began hitting the young man in the back, everybody laughing because he wasn't hurting him—so we thought. Until the younger one shouted, "you want some more?" Turning around he begins to swing as blood begins shooting out of his back, his back opening up to the white meat, blood everywhere. Youngster takes off running down stairs to the officer. The officer sees the blood, closes his door and directs the youngster to medical. You're wondering why the officer closed the door, because, there are men walking around in population with contagious diseases. Hmm, not to mention men having sex with other men who they know or might suspect have HIV or full-blown AIDS. Man, this is a fact of life in prison, think about it. Men who have been locked down for so long in this environment lose all sense of reality and even dignity.

But getting back to the fight, nobody knew at the time, the older gentlemen was hitting him wildly in the back with a razor in his hand slicing youngster's back wide open. Guards coming from everywhere, "Everybody to the TV room!" they yelled. There was blood everywhere. The Guards were looking for the razor as they took the older guy to the hole. The investigation began with each inmate, nobody saw **nothing** and nobody heard **nothing,** we were locked down all day! This is one of the reasons for not coming to this place.

Chapter 3: Deacon

When you look at prison as a whole, everything that they have out here and on the streets they have in prison in some kind of form—the keyword is that it's in a form—it's not real. You have to understand that when a lot of things take place in movies and they give portrayals of what prison may be like; nothing can prepare your mind for what this place can be like. Especially being there doing time year after year, when you don't see any light at the end of the tunnel.

I've heard grown men cry and you can hear them at night.

There are times when you lay in your bed wishing you weren't alive just to escape the pain. There are other times when you wish you would have made the right choice or think, man I wish I hadn't done this (your crime). I've heard grown men cry and you can hear them at nigh especially, when you're in the hole. It's not a place for those who have no understanding of what life is truly about when it comes to being in there. I found myself having the understanding that I had to take care of myself. I got on a bus going to another penitentiary also in Colorado and some of the guys that got on this bus, I'm talking about were on "swole." I'm thinking after seven or eight years that I'm alright by now. I was weighing about a buck 50 when I arrived and at this time I was weighing about 175 to 180. Going to the place that I went to though these guys were huge. This was the first time that I was actually scared and afraid at the same time. These dudes were men who had been locked down for some time and were being transferred to this other joint, which was a medium joint, but a high security joint all the same. I thought being in shape was just running and doing push-ups but I soon saw that it was much more than that.

In this environment that you're in you have to take care of yourself because everyone else is. If you are weak or are not prepared for what is coming your way man you can be vulnerable. Like I said, you have to check all your guns in Receiving and Discharge when you come in. In prison, though they use knives. And you quickly learn how to use one or end up dead.

My first life and death situation was at the first facility that I was at. Not understanding about prison it was my first or second year being incarcerated. My friend was talking to another guy and I interrupted the conversation. The other gentlemen said, "Ok let me finish talking to my guy," and I was like, "man beat it," you know being disrespectful, not understanding fully what I was doing. An hour later somebody came and told me that there was a guy standing upstairs waiting for me with a knife ready to kill me. When I heard that, I in a sense was scared but knew that I couldn't show fear. I went to my friend and asked him what that was all about. I learned that the guy had been locked down for 20 years and basically felt that I had disrespected him. As a man at this time in my life I didn't duck any rec so I went and got a knife, knocked on his door and he said to come in. He said "come in and close the door." I said, "No that's alright, I just came to you as a man to apologize for any disrespect that I may have caused you." He said, "Youngster I was just sitting here on the bed and something was telling me not to do anything to you. I don't know what it was but I was hoping that you would come and apologize." I felt such a relief at that moment. I've seen a lot of things take place being

You'll find a lot of gentleman in this place with nothing to lose.

there. That was my first life or death situation. This older gentleman who became one of my best friends at the time, I saw him get into a fight with a guy who had a razor and he had a knife. I saw him stab this guy at least about 12 times and never got touched with the razor. He basically put work in on my man. He was doing life in prison and he had nothing to lose, he was never getting out.

You'll find a lot of gentleman in this place with nothing to lose. Some have matured to a point in their lives and help other younger brothers realize the error of their ways. Some have become institutionalized, basically never wanting to go home. It's a sad thing. I remember working up on the hospital floor and they had old guys who were doing life plus 50 years. Guys, who were in their 70s, doing stretches of time dying in prison. I remember how we used to put them in body bags and how the police would put handcuffs and shackles on them even in their body bags—that disturbed me. As I look back that was their only way of being free. It was something that helped me to understand that I didn't want to die in prison and I didn't think anybody else deserved to. I remember the older guys that I used to take care of, getting compassionate releases, where basically it meant that they were so old that they couldn't do any harm any more or that they were terminally ill or expected to be dead in maybe three to six months. The sad part of it is that when they would give them these releases they wouldn't have any family members that would want to take them and take care of them so they ended up staying and dying in prison anyway.

Those situations that I saw helped me to always stay humble even though I've gotten into a lot of fights. Some things right now are not prevalent in the story. I've seen a lot of fights, a lot of gang fights, a lot of people getting hurt; some things that I can't even talk about based on confidentiality. But I have to share this, speaking of not wanting anyone to get hurt. One day I'm in the hole, (don't remember what for) in a 6-man cell. We hear a commotion coming down from the hallway, someone sticks a mirror out the window as we hear a voice cry out, "put those mirrors back in" as you see men pulling mirrors back into their chuck holes. We see five guards carrying a Latino man down the hallway, he's spitting and cussing. The Latino men on the range are hollering and cussing. The Captain is walking behind them, a big Indian about 6'5, every bit of about 300 lbs. or more, shouting, "Take him to the end cell!" The range in the hole consists of about twenty 6-men cells to the left and the right of you. Saying to myself, "I know they not gone do that"—But they did. Put him in that cell with six big white boys who represented a gang who got into it with a gang of Latino men. The Captain hollers out, "Get back to the wall!" as he shouted into the room while opening the door. Usually they handcuff everyone in the room, not this time. They threw him in the cell, slammed the door shut and walked away. You heard a scuffle and then moans all night. They left him in there from 4pm to 10 o'clock that night. When they pulled him out, they tore all his clothes off and they brought him down the hall on a stretcher, Latino brothers going crazy, knowing that their homeboy just got raped. Somebody's going to die tonight! And sure enough, two white boys were stabbed up that night. Come to find out, the Latino brother spit in the Captain's face—**wrong Captain to spit on**. This one's vicious, runs the prison and knows he does. The biggest gang in the prisons? THE GUARDS!

But this kind of life I wouldn't wish upon anyone like I said before. Being in

Chapter 3: Deacon

prison there are also a lot of activities that you may want to participate in but most of them bring about trouble. Even with sports knowing that all men are

I remember an old guy would always tell me that 'every fight ain't yo fight and everybody's fight ain't yo fight'.

competitive it usually brings about a fight. In these kinds of places you can't afford to duck any rec. I had to quit playing basketball. I was pretty good at it and really loved the game, but I had gotten to a place in my life where I was living for the Lord and thought I was mature enough to handle someone talking crazy to me. I guess I was wrong because I remember a young guy I was playing against on the court. This day was really just my day, I didn't miss a shot. My man began to talk real greasy to me—cussed me out and some other stuff. At this time I was probably about 12 years in on my incarceration and getting short. I remember an old guy would always tell me that *every fight ain't yo fight and everybody's fight ain't yo fight.* But this day, I had friends on the sidelines and then guys from my home town respecting who I was and what I stood for, but still understanding the laws of prison, looking at me like why haven't you punched my man in the face yet?

I was really trying to give youngster the benefit of the doubt. Well he went on and finally he said something about Jesus and some kind of "jail-house" religion that all people think inmates get when they're in prison. They don't understand that they have real life experiences with God just as people on the street do. That kind of pushed my button based on my love for Jesus and that was all it took. I whooped the sleeves off my man. I really felt bad about it afterwards and as a man went to apologize to him. In the place where we were at though you had to stand on what you truly believed in. Some things you just can't allow because someone else may see it and think that they can get over and do the same thing that another person did. Prison life is all about respect; respecting the next man in every area of his life. It's so sad that we don't have that same respect for one another out here on the streets.

This is a bad place to be. There are people who deserve to be here—I must say that. I think that the criminal justice system has it all backwards where people can molest, abuse and kill our kids—even kill one another and do less time than a person who sells drugs. I'm not saying that drugs are right, but I don't understand the scales of balance. I remember looking at the lady who wears the blindfold, who holds the scales of justice, and I believe that those scales are not weighted correctly when it deals with mankind as a whole right now. That is why her eyes are covered. Murder! Man it depends on who you kill whether you do a certain amount of time or not; but when it comes to drugs and drug laws everything was based on assumption and not fact. It was a strategic plan to fill the prisons up and make money.

Today it is a form of modern day slavery in my opinion and theory. When you can lock up a man and get $25-35,000 a year for him—it would be cheaper for our government to send these men or women to college instead of placing the entire burden on society through taxes and other extremities. I'm looking at my own race and the statistics are astounding. 1.46 million Black men out of a total voting population of 10.4 million have lost their rights to vote due to felony convictions in the United States. Blacks account for only 12% of the U.S. population but 44% of all prison inmates in the United States are black. These statistics are astounding and I believe that it's time that we wake up. This is one of the sole purposes of me writing this book, to save a posterity alive.

I understand we progress through change, so if we are meant to change and progress in life it starts with our children. As I love mine I know that you love yours. Whether they're 5, 10, 15, 20, or 25—love your children. This is the change that we need. As Jesus declared, "such is the kingdom of God." We've been mentally brainwashed into thinking that this is a condition that we need to stay in while we kill one another not understanding that this is a form of genocide. I remember hearing the phrase on the news, "Black on Black" crime. But you've never heard of white on white crime and its happening every day. So looking and having an understanding pay attention and be aware.

As I go back into the story, my release is coming up. Time seems to have slowed down. Some say a usual occurrence when you're ready to go home. After doing almost 13 years flat—should have been out in 12 and half years on my original date—but because of my loss of good time I had to do all the way to my end date. If I knew then what I know now—or shall I say if I would have known better then, I'd be in a different situation. But still release is release. I can't wait to see

Based on my predicament it seems no one came to see or ask about how I was doing as far as my family.

my wife to hold her again, to be with my children, my family, the one that I made. Right now in my life probably the only family that I have. Based on my predicament it seems, no one came to see or ask about how I was doing as far as my family. Like I said before, God has delivered me of all malice or anything that may have hindered me from forgiving those who I felt may have done me wrong. I had to accept that I had done this to myself no one else was responsible. "It was me O Lord." I had to take responsibility for my actions and it was one of the things that helped me to accept and receive my deliverance.

But it's my day. In prison sometimes you have to keep your release date to yourself because there are people who are envious and jealous that may try to cause trouble for you or cause you to get into a fight so that you may lose your date and get it pushed back maybe 30 to 60 to 90 days. I don't understand that concept of why brothers do that. When I saw someone going home, man it was a relief and it meant that I was getting closer. The thing that hurt me the most was seeing people coming back with astronomical amounts of time after doing 10 or 15 years, understanding that this time they would never get out again. So I say this to say that being released from prison was something that I had always dreamed of but right now I'm nervous and I'm a little afraid. Not understanding what I might encounter. I don't know how my children will react to me being home after being gone for so long, or having to understand the emotions that I may have caused not being there. Because I understand that a father has a very important role in raising his children. Although I raised mine from a prison cell— and I didn't do a bad job along with my wife who really did a great job—God blessed me. Upon my release I pray that he may see me through all the things that I may encounter on my way out.

Chapter 3: Deacon

Wisdom Cries: Things to think about!

63% of youth suicides are from fatherless homes.
90% of all homeless and runaway children are from fatherless homes.
71% of all high school dropouts come from fatherless homes.
85% of all youth sitting in prison grew up in fatherless homes

These statistics translate to mean that children from fatherless homes are five times more likely to commit suicide, 32 times more likely to run away, 20 times more likely to have behavioral disorders, 14 times more likely to commit rape, nine times more likely to drop out of high school and 20 times more likely to end up in prison.

Of Black males born this year, 29% can expect to spend some time behind bars. One in 14 Black children has a parent in prison. For every three black men in college, four are in prison.
Only 41% of Black Men graduate from High School in U.S. Out of a total voting population of 10.4 million Black Americans, 1.46 million of them have lost their right to vote due to a felony conviction in the United States.

Thoughts of A Man Locked In the Hole!

- Never make what's wrong, right. A real man walks away from something he strongly desires, to please the God whom he really loves.

- Must learn to walk with endurance along with discipline.

- Lukewarm-ness is your enemy!

- Breathe on me Lord.

- The earth is under a shroud of fear and doubt which is growing thicker and darker- must break through the fear and doubt.

- The wisdom and humility you possess is more important than power, without them power will corrupt you and you will be used for evil!

- Stronghold: A mindset impregnated with hopelessness that causes the believer to accept as unchangeable something that he/she knows is contrary to the will of God.

Chapter 3: Deacon

- I've learned that what often disqualifies us in people's eyes is the very thing which qualifies us for the grace of God.

- We live in a day of great wonders!

- I've learned when something seems impossible the Lord is about to move!

- You don't have to understand to obey, but when you obey understanding comes to you!

- Life grows with interaction that is why on the earth patience must be joined to your faith or you will miss the timing of the Lord!

- Fear makes you weak.

- When you love the most wretched and the most worthless even those in the grips of the darkness then my word of redemption is truly established in your heart.

- You are here because you have learned to see.

- You must receive my word into your heart first then it will open your mind. If you only receive it into your mind it will not live!

Chapter 4
"Darren"

As I progressed through the story you've seen that my name has changed in each episode of my life. I've come to understand that life is not just given to you. Sometimes you have to take what you want. And what I mean by that is that you have to give an honest effort to always do what is right and what is good. As I walked out the door of that prison, I look back on all the men that I had left behind, wondering what would be their outcome. For some strange reason I didn't want to leave them behind even though I knew that was out of my hands.

Getting out of prison I had to go to the halfway house in Leavenworth. I was given a five year sentenced probation after doing 13½ years which I thought was too hard. Transitioning back into society was so strange. Not understanding that everything was just moving too fast for me. In there you had time to sit down and think about what you would do. Out here you don't have time to think so you must plan ahead and ask God to give you direction. This probation thing was too hard on my family and on me and I couldn't do it. I had a choice to stay on probation for five years or to go back to prison. It wasn't about the five years' probation, it was really just about me being free.

There's no such thing as being halfway free, either you're free or you're not and that was my understanding of it. After having a long hard talk with my wife making one of the hardest decisions that I could ever have made I chose to go back. They gave me chance after chance finally sending me back in front of the judge. The courts were asking for 18-30 months on violation. Being that I was under the old law I knew that they could only give me six months to a year; and after doing 15 years, six months or a year was nothing and that was my perception—I don't advise that for anyone else. The judge took his time in deliberating and finally gave me 12 months flat, that way I couldn't get good time or anything. A year and a day I would have had good time. But God graced me.

> *There's no such thing as being halfway free, either you're free or you're not and that was my understanding of it.*

They sent me to South Dakota and I stayed there my time, my last nine months of incarceration. One of the toughest moments in my life that hurt me the most was when my father had gotten real sick and my sister had to put him in a nursing home. While I was out during my release before I went back, I went to see him every other day. I didn't like seeing my father in a home but he had gotten worse in his mind and in his health. I remember when he was younger he had caught gangrene in his leg and they had to cut his leg off. The poison from that leg had gone to the other leg and they had to cut that leg off. The first leg I believe in my heart took all the fight out of my father. He just wasn't the same after that, in his mind, his health or anything. When they took the second leg it was though he gave up and I knew that this was not my father. Looking back sitting in that place, (prison) something left me one day and I felt it when it left me. I didn't know what it was, but it was the life of my father that was inside of me. I have memories but there is something about life that connects you. He passed away and I was 30 days to the door. They wouldn't allow me to go and see him at his funeral—not that I wanted to—but I just wanted it to be my choice. Based on some things that I had done in the past it kept me from going. Hmm, funny how the past still haunt us if we make bad choices.

At the cost of my father's death it still hurts me some today when I think about it. But I move on. He was a part of my life and when he left I felt it. They called me to the counselor's office. I had already in my heart and in my spirit known that he had passed away. The counselor looked at me and asked me how I knew as I told him, "my father must have passed away." He looked astounded. But I knew and he was just confirming what God had told me already. It hurt me and I still haven't really truly grieved over that. That was my father who raised me all the way until he passed away. I miss him to this day; the wisdom that he gave even when he was not his self. He always came to his self when he talked to me. I was always the one that seemed to reach him. Now that he's gone, man I wish he was here. After my release from South Dakota and doing 30 days at Bates County, I was finally released a "FREE MAN".

Now in my life though, God is doing a new thing. I've grown and God has blessed me. I belong to a wonderful church, Harvest Church of Kansas City, MO where Pastor Steve Houpe is the Pastor. He's my spiritual mentor and my spiritual father. I can truly say that he is a blessed man of God and he reminds me a lot of my pops so it wasn't hard for me to truly submit to him. As I watched him over the years he's proved his work. I thank God for a man of God and his wife who has helped him be the man that he is. Thank you Dr. Donna Leah Houpe.

My wife and I are going on 26 years in marriage and it's been a blessing—she's been a blessing to me.

As I enter into life I'm still a little behind technology. But technology seems to have a way of catching up with you. My life is better now than it has ever been. God has given me all the things that I have desired, more than the things that I had when I was in the world selling drugs or anybody else selling drugs. He did a great thing in my life. My wife and I are going on 26 years in marriage and it's been a blessing—she's been a blessing to me. All of my children are doing great and have been a blessing to my wife and me. They're all grown and living their lives now. That was one of my things when I came home just wishing that everyone would stay home for a minute so that I could enjoy their company. But I had to understand that they were older and some of the things that they had gone through without me being there prepared them for this moment. I believe that they're a lot more mature than I give them credit for; but that's just a daddy's love and protection. My wife to this day is still the beautiful person that she's always been—always being a blessing to me. And to you my readers this book is from my heart. It is written to bring wisdom and to save a posterity alive. It is time to change and the change must start with us. We must stop shifting the blame to the white man or any other man. We must look at the man in the mirror and say that enough is enough and say it's my time to prosper, it's my turn.

To be honest I wouldn't be a man of God if I didn't tell you there are a lot of ways to God that seem right to a man but for me the only way that worked is Jesus Christ. He's my Savior and my Lord and He has been blessing me tremendously in my life. I am an entrepreneur with a passion for the lost and our kids however old they may be. I love children. One of my endeavors is to reach as many kids as I can through God's love. With his help I'll make it. I just want to thank God today that I'm living in my best days and I pray that you will too, in Jesus' name.

Wisdom Cries: Things to Think About!

God setteth the solitary in families he bringeth out those which are bound with chains. But the rebellious dwell in a dry land!
Psalm 68:6 (KJV)

And I will restore to you the years that the locust hath eaten, the canker-worm and the caterpillar and the paler worm have eaten...and ye shall eat in plenty. And be satisfied and praise the name of the Lord your God that hath dealt wondrously with you: and my people shall never be ashamed!
Joel 2:25a-26

For perhaps he therefore departed for a season that thou shouldest receive him forever!
Philemon 1:15

Chapter 5
"The 7 Principles to Help You Survive"

Wisdom Cries:

This is for those who may have trouble dealing with incarceration in any form. Also, for any man or woman facing life's obstacles. These principles have helped me through life and as most principles, they are lavished with truth and put together to give insight, direction, and overall peace!

PRINCIPLE 1: THINK

The first principle is something that we should have done before we got to this place. Let's take time to **think**. God says in his word, as a man **thinketh** in his heart **so is he (Prov. 23:7)**. Take inventory, search your heart, ask yourself who am I and where am I going? How did I get here, how can this situation benefit me, what about my kids, how can I leave them a legacy, how can I change this situation? There are many more questions that we could ask ourselves. As you continue to read on **think** about every principle that you encounter. All of these principles are lavished with truth and a man of principle has success in everything that he does—so **think**. And while you're **thinking** fix your thoughts on what is true and good and right, like your kids. **Think** about things that are pure and lovely like your mother or wife, or dwell on the fine, good things in others. **Think** about all you can praise and thank God for and be glad about it, just being alive to be in your right mind is a blessing. And I know it's hard at times, that's when you thank God the most. All of this has to do with your **thinking**. What have you been **thinking** about? Good or bad? Hmmm. You must understand **thinking** is a form of discipline, a form of progress something we take little time to do. It prepares you for action through your thoughts which creates vision—and vision, which brings reality—based on your will to succeed! So take time out to be lavished with truth and **THINK**!

And as a man **thinketh** in his heart so is he **(Proverbs 23:7) KJV**

WISDOM CRIES: Men of Wisdom and how they **think**!

1. *Jesus the Christ:* "it is written, Man shall not live by bread alone, but by every word

that proceeds from the mouth of God!" **(Matt. 4:4 KJV)**

2. ***Martin Luther King Jr.***: "Rarely do we find men who willingly engage in hard solid **think**ing. There is an almost universal quest for easy answers and half-baked solutions. Nothing pains some people more than having to **think**!"

3. ***Emiliano Zapata***: "It's better to die on your feet than to live on your knees!"

4. ***John Kennedy:*** "There are those that look at things the way they are and ask, why? I dream of things that never were, and ask why not?"

5. ***Malcolm X***: "I'm the man you **think** you are…If you want to know what I'll do, figure out what you'll do, I'll do the same thing—only more of it!"

6. ***Solomon***: "Wisdom is the principle thing, therefore get wisdom: and with all thy getting, get understanding! **(Proverbs 4:7) KJV**

7. ***Dr. Steve Houpe:*** "I have discovered that, after living how I was raised, and after all of the things I was introduced to as a young boy, it takes a real man to walk with God!

PRINCIPLE 2: SEEK GOD

With all that is going on around you I told you to **think**. Looking back on your life you may wonder how you've made it this far.

Like me none of us should have made it but it's by His grace which shines on the just and the unjust. Remember the bullet that missed you by an inch or the bullet that hit *God will* you but didn't kill you. Those guys *change* waiting around the corner and *your life.* something telling you "don't go" that was Him. As you can see after reading my story, Jesus changed my life and kept me safe and sane during those 16 years. He gave me peace and strength to endure. He's doing or has already done the same for because YOU are special in God's sight. He says in **Jeremiah 29: 11-14**,

11 For I know the plans I have for you, says the Lord. "They are plans for good and not for disaster, to give you a future and a hope. 12 In those days when you pray, I will listen. 13 If you look for me wholeheartedly, you will find me. 14 I will be found by you," says the Lord. "I will end your captivity and restore your fortunes. I will gather you out of the nations where I sent you and will bring you home again to your own land." **(NLT)**

You have to understand that God has been watching you and protecting you even in there and more so when you were out in the world. He has an expected end of good for you. Trust him. God will change your life.

PRINCIPLE 3: SELF-BELIEF

You must believe in yourself. I remember growing up my sixth grade teacher told me that I would end up as nothing. God and I proved her wrong. I carried that for so long believing what she had said, which brought many insecurities—especially from being a black woman and a teacher. Many of us had scars from parents and family members who told us negative things. Don't carry it, forgive them. They had no idea what they were saying and definitely didn't know who you belonged to—God Almighty! HE made you despite our mistakes God doesn't make junk! You are fearfully and wonderfully made. Who can argue with God? You can make it. Do you believe enough in yourself to succeed no matter who is or isn't there or, what obstacles you may face? It's truly up to you. So once again **think**.

> *I will praise thee: for I am fearfully and wonderfully made: marvelous are thy works; and that my soul knoweth right well.*
> **Psalm 139:14 (KJV)**

Next to knowing God, a knowledge of oneself is most important to your perception of who you are not who somebody else says you are! **Perception:** the act or faculty of apprehending, by means of the senses are of the mind, cognition, and understanding. Simply put, it's how you view, see and understand you and the things around you. Let's look at "you" who was created by Almighty God. There were no mistakes. You were divinely appointed by Him to be given life. Your mother or father had no idea until God said let there be life. Listen, God said that you were fearfully and wonderfully made, marvelous are your works; and that my soul knows right well **(Psalm 139:14 KJV)**. In the original Hebrew text, the word "fearfully" means, 'with great reverence and heartfelt interest and respect.' The word "wonderfully" means 'uniquely marvelous, unique, set apart.'

So I see why the spirit in King David exclaimed, in Psalm 8:4-5, 4 "What is man, that thou are mindful of him? and the son of man that thou visitest him? 5 For thou hast made him a little lower than the angels, (this word in Hebrew means God spelt with a small "g") and hast crowned him with glory and honor. Meaning God has placed you a little lower than Himself and all of creation has given you great reverence and respect along with God who with heartfelt interest, uniquely made you just like Him—set apart and so marvelous in His eyes/crowned with glory (meaning His presence) and honor (His supernatural Love)!

Listen readers, God see's you so different than you see yourself. God told me two years before I got out of prison that I would "reign as a king coming out of prison" **(Ecc. 4:14)** and I believed it even before the prison doors were open. God called me a king so I started to **think** and act like a king and as I acted and talked like the king God called me, my life changed also. God gave me a new perception of myself and I ran

> *...Look in the mirror, and see just how marvelous you are in God's eyes.*

with it. I believed that if I were a king than I needed the things that Kings have in our modern times and by God's grace He gave me that and more. So, you see I'm actually living like a king called and set apart by God.

Check this out, no man or woman can consistently live in a way that's contrary to the way he or she perceives or sees him or herself! If your perception of yourself is that I belong in jail, I'm a convict, no good, I'll never amount to anything, I can never get ahead, I'm ugly, or I'm too fat. I hate to say this, but you'll continue down that road until you see yourself free, prosperous and healed in your mind and body—the way God sees you! So forget what got you in your situation. Put it on a shelf until the right time, then look in the mirror, and see just how marvelous you are in God's eyes. See yourself the way He does. Stand up straight and say from this day forward, I will see myself created by God—a masterpiece of great wealth, a king or queen of royal decent. "**I am no mistake! I was divinely brought into this world by Almighty God and nothing will stop me when I live according to His perception of me!** "Praise God for you are fearfully and wonderfully made!

PRINCIPLE 4: STUDY TO SHOW THYSELF APPROVED

Now that I'm out I've come to understand that wisdom is the principle thing. Therefore get wisdom and with thine getting, get understanding. Studying is defined as the continued self-discipline applied to achieve greatness. Are you wasting or investing your time? If you want to build wealth you first must build a wealth of knowledge. To the reader, what are your dreams and plans? Don't sit back and let time do you—do time. Master it, make it work for you. Learn all that you can when you can, for as long as you can. While incarcerated I was a barber, plumber, laid brick, personal trainer, a cook and learned numerous other skills. The greatest skill that I acquired was how to seek God through his Word. It has done far more for me than anything that I have ever learned. So as always **think**.

What do you have to offer the outside world? It has to be relevant—it's something touched by God's hand. Remember **think** and know the difference between reading and studying. Studying is a focused determination and a willingness to act on what you have learned. In your life, knowledge should become an addiction. This drug will bring personal success and fulfillment. **Remember, sometimes to meet great men, you have to meet them in a book.** With the over crowdedness of the prison population, all forms of rehabilitation have ceased to exist. This only leaves one option: to self-educate through reading and opening and expanding your mind.

Might I add that wisdom starts with God. He will expand your mind and rid it of its contamination so that it can be renewed by his word. Remember, study to show thyself approved and always pay attention to what you read. If it's not going to enhance your life to growth, than it's a waste of time. Focus on books that bring life to your situation. The Bible is my favorite book.

PRINCIPLE 5: PLANNING

The other day I was driving and I got lost not understanding where I was. I needed direction or a map. But if I would have planned better I wouldn't have gotten lost. That's what you need, a plan. What are you good at? How can you accomplish your dreams and make them a reality? How much time do you have left? And to be honest anything can happen. You can be immediately released based on a technicality. Would you be ready? I've seen it happen. You must have an objective; goals, short and long term. Even daily goals to keep you focused. Now put them into action based on the priority of the

Keep current on the things that you are focusing on and allow God first and foremost to guide your steps.

moment. Don't forget to **think**—always. As you set your goals, write them down, and as you complete them it will energize you to commit to action the rest of your goals.

There will be many distractions so stay focused. From my own experiences, I can tell you that everything was different and new. I had to navigate my way through life as though I was hidden away for such a time as this but not really ready. With all that I thought I knew, some of it became obsolete because of time. Keep current on the things that you are focusing on and allow God first and foremost to guide your steps.

And before I end this principle let me share something I read on the internet the other day by a young lady named Wendy Day from Rap Coalition (about artist's don't make money from record deals). It was very enlightening how she broke down the percentage of the pay rappers receive after their first album or record deal. Check this out in a short version, you must understand the rapper is the last to get paid. First comes the label, the manager (15-20% of all artists entertainment income) the lawyer (by the hour 5-10% of the deal) the accountant (by the hour or 5% of all income) and of course, the IRS (28-50% depending on tax bracket). Not counting promotion cost, clothes to represent image and the like. They say this process (the making of the album) may last three years so when you do get paid, it's only about 12% of all royalties and if you're a group, it's less than that. All this depends on the sale of the album or single.

My point is that I hear a lot of young men who say they want to become a rapper. I don't want to kill your dreams but less than 1% of rappers or emcees make it and those who make it are good at what they do based on the influence, the talent, and over all raw skills. Everyone doesn't have it so while you're planning, plan well. Even those who want to make it in the NBA 1%, the NFL 2.4%, you have people from all over the world competing and only 1% make it or 2.4% of the world's population. That's incredible. So you truly have to be blessed by God at what you do. And while there are a number of truly talented rappers— you know the ones who have great influence—they seem to care less about our young men killing each other. I say this, not understanding them personally but with this form of genocide going on it would seem that they could rap about stopping the killing among our young men based on the influence of the music. Because when artists rap about selling drugs and "flipping birds" or "9", it gives our young men the perception that selling drugs will get them to the top of the rap game. You have to understand these are just songs. The only thing most of them say they are flipping are the CDs you keep buying. **Think** about it. If someone got up publicly on a record and said, "I sell drugs," do you **think** he'd still be rapping? I don't think so. There are drug task forces assigned to every person talking about selling drugs on a CD, underground is the same way. I just pray with all of the killing of our youth that someone would rap about it to make them aware of what they're doing because pretty soon there won't be anyone left to buy their CD! And I mean no disrespect to anyone but the fact is most of our youth look up to rappers and I know they didn't ask for it, but it comes with the fame so help me to help them! And remember, **think** while you're planning!

WISDOM CRIES: Things to think about!

We can make our plans, but the final outcome is in God's hands!
Proverbs 16:1 (MSG)

We should make plans...counting on God to direct us.

Proverbs 16:9 (NLT)

PRINCIPLE 6: KEEPING YOUR MENTAL STATE

This is the second most important principle of them all. Maintaining your mental state with all that's happened and will happen in your life whether free or incarcerated. **Think** about it; at first prisons were built to somewhat rehabilitate a person. A person could learn a trade or go to college to get a degree that they might be an asset to his or her family or to society. That's long gone with the passing of the Zimmerman bill. This bill of plan would take college courses, all forms of entertainment and trade schooling out.

There is no form of real rehabilitation in most prisons so self-teaching and learning is a must.

Anything broken couldn't be fixed—it was just taken out and never replaced. How do they expect you to react, **think** or just live with any sanity? They don't. That leaves it up to you. There is no form of real rehabilitation in most prisons so self-teaching and learning is a must. As I've said, before **think**.

Chapter 5: The 7 Principles To Help You Survive

Prison is designed to break you in every way. I strongly advise you, don't ever come to this place, whether physically or mentally. I lost 16 years of my life and can't ever get it back— practically gave it away watching year after year go by along with my family. Sometimes people and family can come and see you and you can still feel alone. Those who have been locked away for some time know that visits sometimes hurt more than they help because when your people leave, you want to go with them but you can't. The feeling of watching them leave every time can break a man down no matter how strong he **thinks** he may be. Especially when it comes to his kids and his woman—it seems to do something to a man. A man's mentality and emotions get the best of him when family is taken away or separated from him. Something will always be missing inside of a real man and it will gnaw at him until he gives it to God or until his release.

This is just one of the forms of reality that will play tricks with your mind. It will cause you to want to push away everyone that may have potential to cause pain in any form in your life including wife, girlfriend, baby mama, kids, parents, and relatives, by not allowing them to see you or talk with you. This is a deception to keep you alone and bitter causing you not to **think** and you don't need that—so focus. Those people that you're pushing away need you, especially your kids. If you push their mother away how will you see them? Mentally you have to maintain family in heart and mind no matter what has occurred. This is important to your sanity.

As I said, look around you, whether incarcerated or free the battle is for your mind which is comprised of your will, emotions, and intellect and you must maintain this at all cost. Like I said this is just one form of a system designed to break your mindset to keep you from reaching your full potential. You must understand that your freedom is at stake. Why do you **think** they keep building more prisons? They must have some belief that these prisons will be filled. So **think**, if you don't give in to the deception by maintaining your sanity and changing the way you **think**, it could hinder your life. In the 16 years of my incarceration, I've seen men lose their minds. As I've stated before, I was in a prison where they held about 1800 mentally unstable prisoners with numerous conditions, only needing to be classified sane to be sentenced to a term of imprisonment.

Chapter 5: The 7 Principles To Help You Survive

Meaning for example you could stay in prison for 20 years until the doctor says you are able to stand trial. That 20 years you've done doesn't go against your sentence or the time that they would give you for your crime.

I often wondered what would cause a man to relinquish his mind to where he is no longer himself. Pressure, simply put, and some men are not built for this type of pressure. You will see all kinds of things. Don't let these things pressure you into relinquishing your mental state. There is so much more that I could write on this one principle for there are so many forms of mental roadblocks in prison. There are long sentences, being stripped naked, always being chained up and many more. So keep your mental state your life depends on it. Jesus was my answer as I told you before. He kept me as I stayed in his word, steadily renewing my mind to accomplish all that he was calling me to do. So above all else maintain your mental state. As we speak it is estimated to be 350,000 prison and jail inmates who are suffering from mental illness and prisons are not equipped to handle or help these individuals. It is difficult for this person with a mental illness to adjust to prison rules not to mention confinement. Most are put in the hole for years, forgotten, being punished for his or her illness. Isolation and harsh conditions keep them suffering because of a lack of mental health treatment.

America's jails and prisons have become our new hospitals. The only place, America that is, where health care is constitutionally guaranteed behind bars. For many in need of mental health services our nation's prisons have become the provider of last resorts. I've seen sane men and women enter prison and lose their minds. What then do you **think** it would do for a mentally insane man or woman? It's devastating and so very dangerous in this environment. Men walking around just like you and me in prison that at any moment could snap and do something abnormal and for the most part dangerous. This principle I had to live with my whole life growing up with a father who wasn't the same in his mind after getting out of prison. It helped kill him. Then for me to go I had to break that cycle over me and my own sons. All I can say is that God kept me and my mind and that curse has been broken over my children and their children to a thousand generations. So regain any portion of your mind that is lost for that lost portion will cause you not to **see** or **think** clearly.

Chapter 5: The 7 Principles To Help You Survive

Things to think on:

Isaiah 26: 3
People with their minds set on You, you keep completely whole, steady on their feet because they keep at it and don't quit (MSG)

Phil. 4: 6-7
Don't fret or worry. Instead of worrying pray. The petitions and praises shape your worries into prayers letting God know your concerns. Before you know it a sense of God's wholeness, everything coming together for good will come and settle you down. It's wonderful what happens when Christ displaces worry at the center of your life. (MSG)

PRINCIPLE 7: GIVING

Personally I think that this is the most important principle of them all. The success in life that you seek will start with your giving. This seems contrary to your situation because it seems that they took so much from you but in reality you took it from yourself. I know you're saying, "That's not true, it was the

...The choice that landed us behind bars we could have truly avoided with the right decision.

white man, the black man, the system, I'm a product of my environment." All that may be true to a point but it still leaves a choice and we all had one; some we may have been forced into, but the choice that landed us behind bars we could have truly avoided with the right decision.

My point is this: we have to come to grips with responsibility—our own—so that we can quit calling ourselves the victim. If we see ourselves as victims we can never truly be free. Nobody can stop you but you. If you claim the title of the victim you'll always be looking for someone to blame your situation on other than the person you see in the mirror every day. I had to admit I made a bad decision and understand what pain or hurt I may have caused in the process. I gave my life to Christ in the hole of a maximum-security prison. He showed me all the wrong I did and the pain of it. It changed my heart and from that point on I just wanted to do good to outweigh the bad. Meaning, I had sowed so much bad, I didn't want to reap its rewards so I began sowing good:

For if you give, you will get. Your gift will return to you in full and overflowing measure pressed down, shaken together to make room for more and running over whatever measure you used to give, large or small will be used to measure what is given back to you.

-Luke 6:38. (True Living Bible)

So looking back we can all see where we missed it or where we didn't listen and it cost us big. We've all burned some bridges; hurt someone or our family members. Admitting your faults and getting free should be your major concern so that you can start giving or sowing good seeds on your account for all the wrong you've done. If you are not free, you'll stay and play the victim looking for excuses or someone to blame. And listen, sometimes money isn't the only answer especially if you don't have any right now. Your time of just physically helping someone in need is bringing about rewards to your account. As for me when money was funny in jail I couldn't give to all the causes of my heart so I simply gave my time taking care of AIDS and cancer patients and those who were paralyzed and couldn't see. I helped them handle their business while in prison. I had a reputation after a while for doing good and helping those less fortunate. It brought tremendous grace to my life and even blessed my family in abundance as well.

Applying these principles to your life I know will change your life. There's an old proverb, **"There once was a man, some thought him mad, it seemed the more he gave, the more he had."** I'm living this principle right now as I share my thoughts. Everything I have is a result of my giving. Every opportunity, every open door, every blessing from above is because with God's wisdom I give. Let me stress this, wisdom is the key to giving—knowing when, how and in what way. This will help keep you in good stewardship—basically being responsible for what has been given to you. Most importantly reach out to your kids and loved ones, even writing letters to repair any damage that you may have caused. Listen to me readers, if you truly want a life of abundance, give until you don't understand it and watch your life change. Jesus through His spirit used my wife to show me how important it was to give. I would get angry with her for giving a portion of our income to the church and everybody else who needed help. I'd cry out, "They're taking advantage of you!" She'd reply, "So, this is what God told me to do." Man I'd be .38 hot. But the strange thing about it was, we never needed anything and still to this day we practice this principle in our life. Those who know us will testify that God has been good to my family. At first I didn't see it but what I've come to understand is that you can't out-give God. When you give from a free heart, you are building up rewards for you and your family especially your seed—your children, your kids.

So do all the good you can, by all the means you can, in all the ways you can, in every place you can, at all the times you can, to everyone you can, as long as you ever can, do all the good you can. I could go on for some pages on this principle alone. The results of my giving can't be explained, it was as though God was dropping things out of the sky to me and he will do it for you as well, I know it. Are you facing something that you need? Start building on your account. I don't care if you're doing life. Put some good towards that life sentence and watch God move. Or you're feeling like I've done too much wrong for my good to outweigh my bad. Listen, first ask God to forgive you and then forgive yourself. God has a funny way of forgetting our past mistakes when we ask him to with a sincere heart. **Remember, the riches that we impart to others shall be the greatest wealth that we could ever retain.** My brothers and sisters, if you want supernatural favor in your life give until it becomes a part of you. An expression of who you really are, building up treasure for the expectation that you are awaiting. Do this and everything will come to you in its right time.

Wisdom Cries: Things to think on!

Cast thy bread upon the waters for thou shall find it after many days.
                     Eccl. 11:1 (KJV)

Chapter 6
"Manhood vs. Fatherhood"

Wisdom Cries:

And He will turn the hearts of the fathers to their children and the hearts of the children to their fathers. If they refuse I'll come and put a curse on the land!
Mal. 4:6 (NKJV)

Don't you see, children are God's best gift? The fruit of the womb, his generous legacy? Like a warrior's fistful of arrows are the children of a vigorous youth.
Psalm 127:3-4 (MSG)

As I begin to write on this subject my thoughts quickly take flight, remembering and bringing my Daddy's face to light. I miss him. I wish he were here just so I could bless him and love him the way he deserved. But what I miss most is just sitting and talking letting time pass us by; talking about any and everything. I never realized how much I need him in that area right now. As a grown man I now realize that I'm often missing something and it's him (George Brown Jr.) my Pops. And I want you to understand his passing took something from inside of me and as I walk this journey of life, I often find myself without direction that only a father can give His seed. And while we're on this subject, let's get into the matter at hand: Fatherhood vs. Manhood. Since we're talking about my father, let's get into fatherhood and its meaning:

FATHERHOOD:
1. The state of being a father. **2.** The qualities of a father. **3.** The state or responsibility of being a father. 4. The kinship (or paternal) relation between offspring and father.

And as I look at the definition it doesn't match anything that I saw growing up except one (the state or responsibility of being a father). I saw my dad work hard to take care of us and was very protective of us (my brother, sister and I). He didn't tell us all the time that he loved us; he showed us by the things he did and as a man this was what fatherhood meant to me. I've lived my life this way until Dr. Donna Leah Houpe was addressing a topic about the little boy inside every man as she mentioned my Pastor, Dr. Steve Houpe and their walk together in marriage. But unknowingly to her, her words were for me however brief. She only spoke a few sentences, but her words were loud and clear. I had to let go of the past, how I was raised—growing up without a mother and at times a father—to the feeling that no one cared or loved me, why my heart was so callus growing up, trying to understand why our life was so hard. I had to let go and I got delivered that day. I thank God for the Holy Ghost in Mrs. Houpe!

And as I began to let go I came to understand that my Dad did the absolute best that he knew how being raised without his father, my Grandpa George Brown Sr. I look just like him! But fatherhood is much more. As a father I've made some mistakes with my own children. It's not easy and although I had shortcomings I've been equipped by God to be better at raising and directing my children. Did you know when a man has a baby as soon as that baby is born the man's body begins to physically change? His brain becomes heightened with intelligence. He becomes more resourceful,

I've been equipped by God to be better at raising and directing my children.

while improving his ability to handle stress, with more activation in the problem-solving area of his brain. There's a neurochemical called vasopressin whose activity is enhanced by testosterone. This chemical is important when you have sex with your mate. It is released which mellows out stress responses and in marriage, might keep a man from suffering stress related illnesses. This neurochemical along with testosterone causes a man to take risks, still roaming still trying to fulfill his "wild oats" as they say. But when a man's baby is born testosterone levels drop. Men had higher levels of prolactin (meaning the desire for sex subsides) and lower levels of sex steroids after baby's birth. Prolactin is known as the hormone of lactation, (a chemical in breastfeeding milk) but it also seems to influence a new father's responsiveness to his baby's cry while testosterone levels drop making him more sympathetic to his babies with more motivation to protect them. So you see, although the mother has a demanding job in carrying your seed, when the baby is born, it's then your responsibility as the man to care for the child.

So, looking at fatherhood and my father and dealing with the little boy inside, I came to understand even with my own kids that being responsible wasn't enough. I have to show them physically that I love them with a kiss on the forehead or cheek, to a warm embrace; something I didn't get growing up which in today's society is much needed for the emotional side of raising children to let them know they're truly loved. Along with our young and older men

Along with our young and older men some of them have never been hugged or shown affection by their fathers.

some of them have never been hugged or shown affection by their fathers. It's something to be hugged by your dad—the feeling of protection and security. I believe that's why there are young men who are so callous and emotionless. Nobody showed them that they were loved. This is what fatherhood is about—loving our children so they can love themselves. So as always, **THINK** about it! And be the best father you can be wherever you're at. Don't ever take your kids for granted!

Now to the subject of Manhood and its definitions:

MANHOOD:
1. The state or period of being a man rather than a child. **2.** The state or time of being a man or adult male person; male maturity. **3.** Maleness as distinguished from femaleness. **4.** Is used to describe the period in a human males' life after he has transitioned from boyhood, having passed through puberty.

Looking back on my life none of these definitions represent truly what I was taught about manhood. When I was growing up, manhood referred to your penis and how many times you used it sowing your wild oats with as many girls who would let you. Back then, the more women you seduced the more of a man you were—how foolish. Now in today's society manhood is seen as a mentality of who they are and it carries with it a "don't care" attitude that lacks compassion for his fellow man. A don't disrespect me or suffer the consequences mentality. Everyone is to blame, from parents to societal expectations and the influence of the media and music. We give permission for our young men to be hard and callus which they think makes them a man. I read a story about a young girl who laughed at a guy who fell down some stairs. The guy had known the girl for years. He pulled out a gun and shot her because he was being teased. Now the girl is paralyzed from the waist down. How tragic! Where did this mentality come from because it has absolutely no bearing on being a man?

Manhood is a process. It must be taught and developed as a boy grows into adolescence and into a man. It's not a mentality but a way or state of being—a mature way of looking at life— a man of God, humble, strong, full of courage, truthful and trustworthy and most of all responsible. (These are just some of the fragments that develop us into a man.) True, nobody taught us so we must teach ourselves that we may teach our sons. In many cultures, there are ceremonies to induct a boy into manhood. For instance, the Maasai are peaceful people in Kenya and Tanzania but when it comes to rites of passage into manhood, the young warriors must seek out and kill a lion and not a sickly, young or female one. They only hunt capable, large, male lions that have a true advantage in winning seeing that these warriors only have a spear in comparison to the safari hunters with large guns and rifles who manage to get killed by lions every year. The Aborigines of Australia take becoming a man pretty seriously. They send their adolescent boys out into the wild to see if they can survive in the Australian Outback unassisted for six months and when or if, they return, no celebration, just shown simple respect. And there are many different rites of passages in countries all over the world but in our society and culture, the rites of

> *Today, men lack a group or communities of males to initiate them into manhood and to recognize their new status.*

passage have all but disappeared leaving men lost and confused, never sure when and if they've become men.

Today, men lack a group or communities of males to initiate them into manhood and to recognize their new status. We use to say that boyhood lasted until you were 18. Now you see men in their 30s, 40s and even in their 50s who are still in boyhood. We call them playboys because they are still with a boy-like mentality, still playing with things and themselves! I remember when I was young growing up playing with guns and cars, as a boy, that's all we did and we're still playing with guns and cars today as men. You remember the toys your sister played with—the Easy-Bake oven, her dolls, having teatime. **Think** about it. Her toys taught her responsibility—how to cook, care for and even prepare for a family from a young age. So why aren't boys given responsible toys? Hmmm. When I was, a boy I played with guns and knives (I made one out of sticks). What did those toys teach me? Or what are they teaching your sons? It's time to teach our young men about life and their culture wherever they may be from. God has called men to give account. "Train up a child in the way that he should go and when he's older he'll not depart from it!" **(Proverbs 22:6 KJV)**. We must start respecting our seed as I said before; they are treasures in earthen vessels **(2 Cor. 4:7 KJV)** fit for the Master's use.

Wisdom Cries: Things to think on!

- *According to the U.S. Census Bureau, 24 million children (one out of three) live in a home absent of a biological father.*

- *A child with an absent father is 54% more likely to be poorer than his or her father.*

- *A study of 13,986 women in prison showed more than half grew up without their father*

- *Being raised without a father raises the risk of teen pregnancy, marrying with less than a high school diploma, and forming a marriage where both partners have less than a high school diploma.*

- *Compared to their peers living with both parents, children in single parent homes had an overall 120% greater risk of being endangered by some type of child abuse.*

- ***All totaled the National Fatherhood Initiative estimates the annual public cost of U.S. fathers absent from the family is at 100 billion dollars!***

CHAPTER 7
"Straight Talk"
ABOUT THE AUTHOR

Some things may be somewhat graphic.

As I sat down to write this book I didn't want to revisit the past; but as they say, you don't know where you're going if you don't know where you've been. As I share my heart with a little straight talk keeping it "1000!" I never in a million years thought I'd be doing time in prison, not to mention doing 16 years. Remembering how things happened still is like a dream or as though I was on some game show. *"Come on down, you're the next contestant selected to go to prison!"*

Looking back, the epidemic that shook the United States to its core was crack cocaine. I didn't know anybody that it hadn't affected in one way or another. It was my avenue to prison. During this time in my life I had no value for my life or anyone else's. Just like the Bible says my conscience was seared not knowing right from wrong and not even bothering to care. The only thing that truly mattered was my family—the one that I made my wife, and my kids—and even then those were only mere words. I was taking all of our money and some possessions and spending it on crack. I felt ashamed and left my home for a short time living in the streets sleeping in abandoned cars and dope houses. I walked the streets with a 9 mm pistol with one bullet in the chamber. I was too proud to beg so I took, getting worse and worse. I started robbing dope houses, the most dangerous thing you can do in the streets; I didn't care, nobody was safe, I was raised in the streets and during this time, I barred none. My life was almost taken too many times to count. Somebody was watching over me even in my sin.

Thinking back I recall a guy shooting at me through the wall with a 45 hand gun, at the dope house I was in. I was as good as dead but once again the bullets missed me. Numerous encounters *God was protecting me and someone was praying for me.* like this one were the norm. God was protecting me and someone was praying for me. There were times when bullets would miss me— when something or someone through a small voice would say, "*Don't go around that corner,*" and for some odd reason I'd listen and would come to find out that my life was at stake!

Everything moving too fast for me to **think**, I found myself with a group of gentlemen who were money chasing, selling crack cocaine. It was as though I had gone from bad to worse selling the same thing that kept me in bondage to others, "God have mercy." I woke up one day not even wanting to smoke anymore almost as if I never had in the first place. It was strange; but the sad part was I got addicted or hooked on the power of now selling crack, and everything that came with it. Little did I know though, that time was running out. Everything and everyone around me started encountering trouble of some sort. My best friend was almost killed laying in a coma in the hospital, his head three times its normal size. Some guys had jumped on him and I had just left him five minutes before everything had taken place. It broke me down. I thank God that the police did their job catching the guys because vengeance was mine!

Soon, about a week after this, one of the gentlemen who would later be a co-defendant of mine, was shot in the stomach inside the dope house after getting into an altercation after selling a gun. With so many things like this happening but never affecting me, I now realized my wife's prayers were somehow working. I wasn't a religious man, nor did I have a true understanding of who God was, but I knew one thing; that when my wife prayed for things God heard her. I was going in the opposite direction, her serving God and me serving the devil. I remember my wife telling me five years in, how she would wait for me to go to sleep and anoint my whole body with oil. I'd wake up all oily and sweaty to the point that the spot where I had laid was wet. "What's wrong with me?" I thought, not knowing my wife was praying Legion out of me!

To me my wife's prayers, or answers to prayers, seemed like a coincidence of some sort, not realizing the power of God that was on and in my woman.

While we're on the subject of my wife let me share with you what an extraordinary woman God blessed me with. I met her in high school got married in 1986 probably the best decision in my life besides accepting Christ Jesus into my life. She's endured a lot mentally putting up with me through the years from dealing with my crack addiction to going to prison leaving her alone with three kids. I must admit I wouldn't be the man I am today if not for my wife. She helped me find myself when I was lost with God's help. I think back when I started doing my time how she would tell me God was going to look out for us and make everything all right. I didn't believe her or God for I blamed Him for my demise and you must understand, you **can't attract what you despise.** But she believed in what God was saying in His Word and what her, now our, man of God, Dr. Steve Houpe was preaching—faith plain and simple—she took it and ran with it. She's extraordinary, "weird" is what I'd say sometimes—sort of peculiar—kind and so hospitable but her greatest attribute is loving God and next loving me (with a smile) how could a woman wait 16

I must admit I wouldn't be the man I am today if not for my wife.

years on a man? A lot of people didn't know I tried to push her away so she could be happy the first, the third and the fifth year based on my own insecurities, until she flat out got tired of explaining to me how God would keep her from being sexually promiscuous and how she didn't trust or want another man around our children. Furthermore how she was more afraid of God than she was of me. So, after that we never talked about it again.

I was truly baffled seeing guys tearing phones off the wall receiving Dear John letters from their wives or girlfriends, notifying them of their untimely departure telling them that they couldn't do it anymore. How was my wife going to do 10 more years of this bit with me? I thought it was impossible until I met Jesus in the hole and I came to understand that all things are possible with Him. The more doubt or confusion would try to enter in, the more I believed in what Jesus could do. Though we had our rough moments, and most of it was me, just tired of being without my wife and children. It would get to me, causing me to act ugly for no reason and this woman of mine would always stay humble speaking soft calm words that would melt me like butter defusing any argument I might think about having. You have to understand in this place

When doubt or confusion would enter in, the more I believed in what Jesus could do

called prison everybody's angry at times. Some handle it better than others as I said earlier; you must guard your heart under all circumstances. **The truth is that a man's circumstances do not determine the attitude of his heart but the attitude of his heart, however, may well determine his circumstances**.

Those of you who know someone or will have contact with those who have been locked away, be patient with them. They've encountered more than can be expressed by me or them. From being counted five to six times a day, don't be surprised if your man is standing by his bed waiting on 4:00 count or asking permission to use the restroom, to becoming overly protective of what's theirs, to watching everything and everybody around him, and even to being known by a prison number. 06998-045 was my prison number—your I.D. wherever you went. When I got out someone asked me my name, I had to catch myself from saying Brown 06998-045. These are just a few things mentally you have to deal with not to mention the physical. Being stripped searched everywhere you go, to watching your back from other convicts who might be going through something. It's a fight every day in prison hoping you're not the one who's fighting or who lost. There's no holds barred in there because your life could be taken at any moment from man-made shift shanks. I've seen some as long as a machete. I've seen beatings with combination locks put into a sock tied tight, or getting into a fight with a man who has a razor hidden in his mouth. It's life or death in here.

I saw two gentlemen from Portland get into an altercation one of them a little older, was playing with the other one sexually by slapping him on the butt in front of a room full of men in prison which the young man took offensively to the point of tears swelling in his eyes. Mad with rage, he took off cursing under his breath; me and my

I've seen beatings with combination locks put into a sock tied tight, or getting into a fight with a man who has a razor hidden in his mouth.

cellmate Big D were cooking at the microwave when youngster came up to us asking if he could use it right away. Looking at his demeanor, we let him, as he began pouring baby oil, magic shave, and a broke up snicker, bringing it to a boil, we moved back as he exited the microwave heading around the corner from which he came. We followed to make sure it wasn't for our homeboy. He ran up on his homie throwing it in his face, my man screaming as he held his face, pulling his hands away you saw nothing but the white meat of his hand prints on his face, skin in hands and face melting—youngster whipping him all the while as he took off running for help. Man I saw this.

In prison your manhood is taken extremely serious. Every man wants to leave with his intact unless it's your choice. In prison we called them punks—men who would rather be women to the point of getting sex changes or taking hormone pills. Men with breasts walking around in population (prison), no real man wants this label on him unless he chooses so. I see why youngster did what he did but I might also add youngster received 10 years on his sentence. Was it worth it? Yes and no. "Yes" because if he didn't do anything about it, everybody else would have thought it was ok to slap youngster on the butt becoming a lamb among wolves, and "no" getting 10 more years and having to always watch your back is too stressful. So you see, these are just a shadow of all the things we're dealing with; so be patient and understanding with the one you love, for he loves you too, he just doesn't know how to show it yet. If you personally know someone in prison go see them, write them letters just to say hi, it will mean more to them sometime than the money you may send.

I've been out for about five years now and life is moving at a rapid pace. I had to adjust. My family seemed to be moving 100 miles per hour. I'm just now getting my bearings. When I first got out I didn't know whether to be young or old, I was first arrested at 29 and was completely free at 45. I missed all of my 30s in prison. How will family react to my release? Will my children even know who I am? Has my woman been faithful? These were some of the questions I asked myself and you will too. Will I be able to find a job? Who will hire me after 16 years in prison? God was faithful to all of the questions I asked myself. The one I wanted to know the most? Was my wife faithful? And as a man, "you know," God was faithful to His word and kept her. As I said before, she's extraordinary. I had to ask myself how did she do it? She told me she fell in love with God (Jesus) and that He was her husband while I was away. In my natural mind I didn't want to believe it, based on the

...When I first got out I didn't know whether to be young or old, went in at 29 got out at 45.

things I heard men saying about their women. But a man knows his woman and I thank God for her because she had every right to leave according to the world's way of looking at things and based on my past errors. Man, she had the right to do whatever she wanted. But my woman doesn't look at the world's way but God's way and here we are going on 26 years of marriage. We've been together for some 31 years now living in our best days.

As I share these thoughts with you, God has poured out blessings on my life and the life of my children as well. I'm not going to sit here and front and say this didn't affect my family. It did—mentally and emotionally. I thank God for strong children who welcomed me despite some of their inner feelings which we addressed. I did a lot of apologizing but I had to understand that I couldn't make up for time lost. I wish, oh how I wish I could turn back time, but I can't and sometimes I feel guilty for cheating my wife and kids out of a life without me. But God is faithful. He has restored and given me my heart's desires and more and He'll do it for you as well. It's time for us men to take our rightful place wherever we may be—in our homes and in the lives of our children. This is right and we must not take no for an answer. Our women need us, our sons need us, our daughters need us and society needs us.

> ***Men of renown, men of valor, Kings in the sight of God; walk in your rightful place!***
> **Jeremiah 29:11-14 (MSG)**

In Conclusion, with all that I've said and shared with you, looking around THINK for a moment; how this message can benefit you. And to my brothers in prison "THINK!" They can't lock up your mind. With all that's going on, it's hard, but the words on these pages I've written as I went through much pain and adversity, served to teach and mature me by not keeping me in darkness. **Hebrews 2:10** says, Christ learned by the things he suffered; His pain was His teacher and our experience however painful should serve to teach and motivate us to our rightful place. For out of prison He cometh to reign! **(Ecc.4:14)** And that reign starts with our children who are killing each other. We have to stop it. No one else can, it's up to us. Reading "The Call" paper, a black-owned newspaper established in 1919, I came across an article put out on Trayvon Martin's death, the young man who was gunned down on the streets of Florida. Although so very sad, his death is not unique. In 2008 and 2009, 2,582 Black children and teens were killed by gunfire. Black children and teens were only 15% of the child population, but 45% of the 5,740 child and teen gun deaths in those two years. Black males 15 to 19 years old were eight times as likely as white males to be gun homicide victims. The national outcry over Trayvon was right and just. But we need the same sense of outrage over every one of these children's deaths; we need a sense of pride and self-respect. Guns are the major cause but guns don't shoot themselves—it takes people—and although tougher gun laws need to be enforced we need to teach our kids common sense and self-pride. To love oneself and the next man the same.

...We need a sense of pride and self-respect.

As I said before, the purpose of this book is to save a posterity alive here on this Earth! And it starts with saving our children. So, join with me, let's take back our city and the block and snatch our sons and daughters from the enemy's hand. May God bless the hearer and reader of this book with all spiritual blessings in heavenly places in Christ Jesus, My Lord and Savior's name!

Letters

In this section of the book you will find letters written to help you outline your own personal thoughts or feelings to your children and even to God. While you may of course change the content somewhat, it is my prayer that they serve as good starting points to **think** on.

A Letter of Salvation to God!

"Hi God"

When I was growing up I would hear people talk about you, wondering who they were talking about and where did you live? I heard it was in heaven, they say you have mansions up there for those who believe in you. That sure sounds nice. The house that I grew up in was kind of small and we lacked a whole lot of things, like water, food, and lights. I want to ask you God why was that? I'm hoping that I can one day make it up there to see you. I want one of those mansions they talk about. Hey by the way there's this book called The Bible they say You wrote it and that it changes lives and its alive. How is that possible? I think I need to read this book, my life isn't going so well right now. I've made some bad choices and I'm going in the wrong direction, they say you can help me. One day when I was younger my grandmother took me to this place called church. It was ok. This preacher kept talking about Jesus. He sounds like a great person. Is He Your Son? I remember Him saying how Jesus died for us. Why did He do that? He must really love us. Is Hell real God? They say it is and it's real hot down there—I guess down there if Heaven is up with you God. You know what God—I'd better read Your book so that I can know more about You. Do you know everything? If You do then you know what kind of trouble I'm in. Could you help me? They say there is nothing too hard for You and I have nothing to lose right now. I'm kind of in a hard place. I'm trying to believe—please help my unbelief. If your Son, Jesus died for us, even me, I need You. I've never felt this alone in my life. Please don't pass me by God. Send your Son Jesus to change my heart and mind. All of my choices have led me to this point. God, they say that the Bible says all I have to do is believe in your Son and I'll be a part of you. They say you never lie. I can't wait to meet you. Please don't let me down. A lot of people have, but for some reason I don't believe that you will. Thank you and I hope to hear from you soon!

Love ya man

A Letter To My Son

Hi_____

First off I want to say I love you man and I miss you. How's my son doing? Fine I'm sure, your mother is a good woman and she's doing a great job raising you so always look out for your mom! She tells me you're getting big. I haven't seen you in a while and it hurts. I guess you're wondering where Daddy's at? Well, I'm in grown up time out. Sort of like when you do something wrong and your mother says go to time out. Well, Daddy did something wrong so I have to stay in time out for a little while. Well enough about me. Your mom says you're really smart and son I don't know if you can read this letter or not, if not, have her read it to you. Daddy just wants to share his heart with you. When you were born I was so proud—the most blessed man alive and I promised myself you wouldn't live or grow up like I did alone and poor. Right now I feel so bad for breaking my promise, leaving you and your mother to fend for yourselves. Son, I'm sorry, please forgive me. I never meant for any of this to happen, I just wanted a better life for you. I lost my way moving too fast never taking time out to **think** about how all of this would affect my family and my children. As I sit here mad at myself for allowing me to be deceived in such a way. That's why as long as I have breath in my body I will always as you mature tell and share the truth with you, which I know will keep you free. Son I met a man named Jesus and He showed me all that was wrong with me and how much love He showed by fixing everything that was hindering me. I believe that my life will take a drastic turn for the better. He even taught me to pray, something that's so important that I never took time to do. The other day I prayed that Jesus would watch over you and your mom, your sister and brother too. Son, I feel so confident that He will that I just began to thank Him. He's awesome! He's taught me a lot mostly to stop being so angry and to forgive those who may have wronged me even to asking forgiveness from those I hurt. It's important Son to treat others the way you want to be treated. Your life will be a lot easier. And one day when you're old enough to understand I will introduce Jesus to you. He gives me so much peace and will do the same for you my son. _____ I want you to always remember, family comes first next to Jesus. Always look out for and protect your mom and sisters. It's no pressure son just do your best that's all that matters. Son, there's so much more I want to share with you but I'll have to write it in the next letter. I love you Son and hope to see you soon!

P.S. Tell your mom and sisters Hi and I love them for me. Thanks and never forget you are a reflection of me, your daddy, and I am a reflection of you my son!

Love ya man

Daddy

A Letter to My Daughter

Hi_____

     How's my beautiful daughter? Before you say I'm good let me shout for the world to hear that I love you _____ and Daddy misses you so very much. As for me, I'm doing just fine and by now you've figured out where Daddy is. I'm so sorry for hiding it from you. Please forgive me I was trying to protect you from any embarrassment. As I sit here writing I think it's me that I'm trying to protect, not wanting anybody to know your daddy's in jail. I don't know what I was **thinking**—that's just it, I wasn't thinking—and I left you unprotected trying to do something that was totally wrong. I was deceived into believing that you can get something without having to work for it. Always remember baby girl that nothing in life is free. It seems everything has a price on it in this world. So I heard you're in school and you're really smart, on the honor roll already. Daddy's so proud. So how do you like it (school that is)? Do you have any new friends? I'm sure you do. And by the way, I plan on going back to school too. I think it's about time. I have to change _____. A friend introduced me to God the other day. I learned that His Son Jesus died for me and you, not to mention the whole world. I'm still trying to figure out how He did it, dying for people He didn't even know. I think that He must have loved us so very much; kind of like the love I have for you right now. Jesus has given me a new perspective (I know that's kind of a big word) it just simply means I see things a little different right now. I've been praying for you and your mom that God would bless you with all the desires of your heart that are good for you and that He would watch over you always. Daddy hopes to be home soon so I can take you on your first date. You're probably wondering, "what's a date?" Well, it's when your Dad (me) takes you out to a fancy restaurant or just to the ice cream shop to treat you like the princess that you are. Whatever your desire from opening doors for you to pulling out your seat, even making sure you're not too cold or too hot—your wish is my command because you deserve the very best and the very best is what you'll have in Jesus' name. So get ready I'll be home soon. And by the way, stay away from boys they have the cooties ☺. I don't know what that is but stay away it might get on you and Dads don't have cooties so you can hang with me! Anyway _____ remember Daddy loves you and write me soon. Your letters make me happy which causes me to smile so big I can't stop! P.S. Tell your mom and brothers Hi!

Love ya Babygirl,
Daddy

DARREN BROWN
Author, Entrepreneur, & Community Activist

Darren Brown was born and raised in the heart of Kansas City, MO, in an impoverished and dangerous upbringing abandoned by his mother at six years old and rescued by his grandmother. Living an unsupervised life, caught in poverty's grip, Darren knew that life had more to offer than struggle, which led him to the streets of Kansas City at 11 years old, drawn to the hustle and affluence of the drug game as early as the sixth grade. After graduating from high school and marrying his high school sweetheart, risking his family and his life, he became engrossed in the fast life of drugs, violence, and riotousness that abruptly ended in arrest, regret, and 16 years of imprisonment to pay for.

Through Darren's life changing experience it is his heart, mandated by God, to save a posterity alive here on this earth! Darren's notoriety is most attributed to his new best-selling biography BUG "Straight Talk", a raw 16 year journey through some of the worst penitentiary's in America, and the woman who waited.

Darren is the president and founder of Wisdom Cries LLC, a non-profit organization that endeavors to impact the community through education, awareness, and pure wisdom. As a consultant in prison prevention and intervention, Darren's passion is reaching out to our children and young people through partnerships such as the Kansas City Missouri school district, the KCMO prosecutor's office, and many more. Darren Brown is open to speaking engagements, counseling, and interviews, including schools, men's conferences, and community organizations.

Follow D. Brown on Twitter:

@BugStraightTalk

Or Like him on Facebook:

Facebook.com/dbrown100

The following is a featured foreword that I wrote for my wife's book, "A Woman's Worth." Her book tells the awesome story of how she waited for me while in prison, kept our family, and how God's love can restore any situation and help women know their worth in Christ.

Do you not know I am a woman? I find my circumstances both amazing and powerful. A famous excerpt from Marianne Wilson said it best. "Who am I to be brilliant, gorgeous, talented or fabulous? Actually, who are you not to be?" I deserve absolute respect and acknowledgement. I am the true *shero* of humanity. I am worth the wait, because I understand, "A Woman's Worth!"

A woman's worth is unique in every way. Like a diamond it shines with its many facets giving clarity to its presence. Just as diamonds are rare and unique, there are people in this world who I believe are just like diamonds, divinely placed here on this Earth as though God's plan was to allow Himself to flow, breathe, move and have His very being in them. Although He is just,

God seems to favor abundantly these intricate vessels of purpose; it seems as though they give meaning to life, for whoever comes into contact with them. Because every human life is precious to God, we know that these peculiar, some may think strange creatures are gifts that reflect God's love to mankind, walking and living among us! Let me tell you about one such individual and although I may be a little biased, this beautiful person is my wife whom I've shared 26 years of marriage with. This woman, who gave me such unconditional love and support, endured pain and isolation, she loved me beyond all of my faults, and cried behind closed doors as God gathered her tears in a bottle preserved to produce a river of joy. She fought battles nobody knew about. Suffering that she endured because she believed there was a reason that was worth the effort. While you're reading this you may be thinking what's so special about her suffering? She did it trusting God for 16 years during my incarceration. This is her story of how she kept herself pure trusting in God's all sufficient grace to save her husband from himself and to help him find his way back to God. Do you believe in miracles? If you don't, you will after reading this story.

This book was written with you in mind, perhaps to bring about a miracle in your own life. As a matter of truth, I know this book will change the way you see yourself bringing clarity to life. So, don't just read this book, make it your own. Reflect and consider the thoughts you just read without rushing to the next chapter, because this book will make you want to do that. With that, let every woman and reader around the world brace yourself, find your perfect comfy spot, open up the pages of the this book and be lavished with truth and wisdom that unveils A WOMAN'S WORTH!

Darren Brown

Now Available!

The True Story of a Wife's Love That Upheld a Family & Reached the Depths of a Husband Behind Bars.

A Woman's Worth

An Excerpt:

...Have you ever been physically slapped in the face? I haven't but spiritually I've been slapped a few times. Darren had been gone maybe a year or two. I don't remember exactly, but I was praying to God crying my heart out, "Please give him back I'll do anything, I'll cook, I'll clean whatever I need to do, because he did all or most of the cooking and most of the cleaning along with taking care of the kids. He ironed my uniforms for work a lot of times, bathed me at night when I got home. He literally had my bath water ready and waiting and physically bathed me and put me in the bed. During this time, I was managing a restaurant and I would get home late, some nights 12:30am, 1 or sometimes 2 or 3 in the morning on Friday or Saturday nights. At any rate, I was crying my heart out and I thought that if I started doing some of the things that the woman usually does like cooking and cleaning that God would give him back to me, but as I was balling my eyes out, what I got was a slap in the face. The Holy Ghost said to me, "That's what got you in this mess in the first place, you loved him more than you did me." I said OUCH! I immediately began drying up my tears and as I was wiping my face, I said to the Lord holding my hands up as if He (God) were standing in front of me, "Hold that thought Lord, let me go and search my heart, cause I dare not lie to the Holy Ghost I walked away and about two days later I came back to that exact spot of prayer and said "Lord you were right, I didn't know when you were asking me to keep myself and I thought I couldn't do it that I was placing him before You (God), I didn't realize that I was making him my god and for that I am **eternally** sorry. I can tell you this day though, "I love you more," I said you are the only person who can say, "I'll never leave you nor forsake you and mean it.. I said he wants to be here now, but he's not. You're the only one who can make that promise and back it up, so I say to you that I do indeed love you more. I'll never make the mistake of placing him or anything else before you again...

By Tonya Brown

About Author Tonya Brown

Entrepreneur, Author, and Motivational Speaker Tonya Brown was born and raised in Kansas City, Missouri. Her life tells a story of hope and perseverance that is inspirationally geared towards encouraging women of all ages and backgrounds, but also young men.

At the age of fourteen, Tonya met her high school sweetheart Darren who would prove to play a major role in both her life and her purpose. Upon graduating high school the two had their first child together, were quickly wed, and balancing the life of responsibility and hardship. Tonya's world was turned upside down when her husband was hit with multiple prison sentences for his involvement with drug distribution leaving Tonya to rear their family alone. Forced to deal with a harsh new reality for her marriage and her family, Tonya drew strength from her devoutly rooted faith in God and His ability to sustain not only her husband, but her family and her new role as a "single" woman.

Tonya's unwavering love and prayers for her husband permeated prison bars and played an undeniable role in his radical sell out to Christ. Today the two enjoy the fullness of not only civil freedom but freedom in every area of their lives. They unanimously attribute their successes as entrepreneurs, authors, and community advocates to God's favor and love.

Tonya's sole mission is to help women understand that their value and self-worth is complete only in Christ, whether single, married, divorced, widowed, young or old. Her zeal for life and passion for helping others are remarkably evident in the sharing of personal testimony and service to others. Tonya's bold personality and candidness are as much a part of her charisma as her heart to make an impact on the Kingdom of God.

Connect With Author Tonya Brown!

Twitter:

@mrstonyabrown

Facebook:

Facebook.com/AuthorTonyaBrown

CONTACT
INFORMATION

It is the heart of D. Brown to reach and uplift the hearts of men, women, and of course children both nationally and internationally as well. He and his wife have committed their lives to encouraging and uplifting others to reach their lives' greatest potentials   For more information about book ordering, public speaking engagements, new book releases, social media updates and exclusive prize giveaways log on to:

WWW.WISDOMCRIES.INFO

For ordering, or for more info write or call:

Wisdom Cries LLC
22 E. 32nd St.
Kansas City, Missouri
64111-1106
(816) 561-2809

www.ingramcontent.com/pod-product-compliance
Lightning Source LLC
Chambersburg PA
CBHW051833090426
42736CB00011B/1790